Compulsive Hoarding and Acquiring

Compulsive Hoarding and Acquiring

Workbook

Gail Steketee • Randy O. Frost

UNIVERSITY PRESS

2007

OXFORD
UNIVERSITY PRESS

Oxford University Press, Inc., publishes works that further
Oxford University's objective of excellence
in research, scholarship, and education.

Oxford   New York
Auckland   Cape Town   Dar es Salaam   Hong Kong   Karachi
Kuala Lumpur   Madrid   Melbourne   Mexico City   Nairobi
New Delhi   Shanghai   Taipei   Toronto

With offices in

Argentina   Austria   Brazil   Chile   Czech Republic   France   Greece
Guatemala   Hungary   Italy   Japan   Poland   Portugal   Singapore
South Korea   Switzerland   Thailand   Turkey   Ukraine   Vietnam

Published by Oxford University Press, Inc.
198 Madison Avenue, New York, New York 10016

www.oup.com

Oxford is a registered trademark of Oxford University Press

ISBN-13 978-0-19-531055-9
ISBN 0-19-531055-1

9 8 7 6 5 4 3 2 1

Printed in the United States of America
on acid-free paper

About Treatments*ThatWork*™

One of the most difficult problems confronting patients with various disorders and diseases is finding the best help available. Everyone is aware of friends or family who have sought treatment from a seemingly reputable practitioner, only to find out later from another doctor that the original diagnosis was wrong or the treatments recommended were inappropriate or perhaps even harmful. Most patients, or family members, address this problem by reading everything they can about their symptoms, seeking out information on the Internet or aggressively "asking around" to tap knowledge from friends and acquaintances. Governments and health care policymakers are also aware that people in need do not always get the best treatments—something they refer to as *variability in health care practices.*

Now health care systems around the world are attempting to correct this variability by introducing *evidence-based practice.* This simply means that it is in everyone's interest that patients get the most up-to-date and effective care for a particular problem. Health care policymakers have also recognized that it is very useful to give consumers of health care as much information as possible, so that they can make intelligent decisions in a collaborative effort to improve physical health and mental health. This series, Treatments *That Work*™, is designed to accomplish just that. Only the latest and most effective interventions for particular problems are described in user-friendly language. To be included in this series, each treatment program must pass the highest standards of evidence available, as determined by a scientific advisory board. Thus, when individuals suffering from these problems or their family members seek out an expert clinician who is familiar with these interventions and decides that they are appropriate, patients will have confidence they are receiving the best care available. Of course, only your health care professional can decide on the right mix of treatments for you.

This particular program presents the latest version of a cognitive–behavioral treatment for excessive hoarding behavior. Commonly thought to be a type of obsessive–compulsive disorder, the problem of hoarding can have devastating consequences, not only on individuals suffering from this problem, but also their families and, in many cases, their neighbors and public health authorities, who may be called in when excessive debris and garbage accumulates outside the house. The essence of this problem is the inability to throw away items or possessions that are no longer needed, or necessary. In many cases, houses become so cluttered that it becomes impossible to use the living space in any reasonable kind of way. This problem is estimated to afflict approximately 1% to 2% of the population and, up until this time, no effective treatments have existed. Now, after a number of years of development, Drs. Frost and Steketee have developed the first treatment with strong promise for success. In an evaluation of the latest version of this treatment, individuals reduced clutter in their homes by approximately 50% after just several months of treatment and continue to make substantial progress. These results make this program a beacon of hope for those who have suffered its consequences, sometimes for decades. Although this program must be carried out under the guidance of a skilled clinician who has been trained in its use, it offers the best hope yet of relief from the considerable suffering associated with hoarding.

David H. Barlow, Editor-in-Chief,
Treatments *ThatWork*™
Boston, Massachusetts

Acknowledgments

We are grateful to our families for tolerating our constant work and endless deadlines. Gail thanks her husband, Brian McCorkle, for his understanding and helpful comments. Randy thanks his wife, Sue Frost, for her support and encouragement.

This book would not be possible without the participation of the many people who have sought help from us for compulsive hoarding problems during the past decade. They are too numerous to name, but all stand out because of their compelling stories and their willingness to participate in our research studies. We have learned a great deal from them and have much more to learn. A special thanks is due to the members of the H-C list who have communicated with us in various ways over the years, and in particular to Paula Kotakis, for her dedication to helping people with this problem and helping us sort out how therapists can help. We would like to thank our collaborator Dr. David Tolin and our research team members and therapists, Christiana Bratiotis, Ancy Cherian, Diane Cohen, Amanda Gibson, Krista Gray, Scott Hannan, David Klemanski, Danielle Koby, Terry Lewis, Nicholas Maltby, Suzanne Meunier, Matt Monteiro, Jessica Rasmussen, and Cristina Sorrentino; as well as Robert Brady and Stefanie Renaud, our research assistants, for the insights they have provided in developing this treatment.

Finally, we would like to thank our editors, Mariclaire Cloutier and Cristina Wojdylo, for their tireless efforts to bring this workbook to life.

Contents

Chapter 1

Introduction

Goals

■ To understand compulsive hoarding

■ To learn about this treatment program and what it will involve

What Is Hoarding?

Hoarding can be defined as having three components: (1) the acquiring of and failure to discard a large number of possessions that appear to be useless or of limited value, (2) living spaces sufficiently cluttered so that the clutter precludes activities for which those spaces were designed, and (3) significant impairment in functioning or distress caused by the hoarding. Acquiring problems may be evident in behaviors such as acquiring free items, picking up things others have thrown away, and compulsive buying. Failure to discard includes difficulty parting with unneeded objects (clothing, newspapers, magazines, unsolicited mail, and so on), which leads to excessive clutter in the home. These problems often lead to significant impairment in social, occupational, and financial functioning, and can cause considerable emotional distress. The model on which this treatment program is based assumes that hoarding is associated with three types of deficits or problems: information processing deficits, problems with emotional attachments to possessions, and erroneous beliefs about the nature of possessions. These problems lead to avoidance of decision making, discarding, organizing, and other situations that might trigger discomfort related to hoarding. Hoarding is most commonly considered to be a symptom of obsessive–compulsive disorder (OCD). In fact, checking and cleaning rituals are frequent among people who suffer from compulsive hoarding. We know that hoarding often starts in childhood, and that there is a tendency for excessive saving behavior to run in families. We have very little information about the best way to treat compulsive hoarding. However, this treatment program has shown considerable promise.

Frost and Steketee (1998) provide an overview of the cognitive and behavioral model from which the treatment program for compulsive hoarding is derived. You can access this article through the Obsessive Compulsive Foundation (OCF) website at www.ocfoundation.org. This model holds that hoarding is a multifaceted problem based on several types of deficits or conditions, each with several components. These components are briefly outlined in the following subsections.

Information Processing Problems

Many people who suffer from compulsive hoarding have difficulty making decisions. From major decisions (e.g., job changes) to minor ones (e.g., ordering at a restaurant), people who have hoarding problems often agonize over what to do. These problems are especially evident in decisions about saving and organizing.

Efficient organization of possessions requires the ability to combine like objects into meaningful categories for filing and/or storage. People with a compulsive hoarding problem have difficulty in this regard, perhaps because they see each possession as complex, unique, and irreplaceable. Before discarding, each feature of the object must be considered, and the possibility of finding something this unique again must be estimated. Attempts at organizing/discarding often involve examining an object, only to place it back in the pile of things from which it was drawn. The result is a pile of unrelated objects—both important and unimportant—that get "churned" during attempts to organize and result in "losing" important things.

Difficulties with confidence in memory may complicate the processing of information for people who hoard. They often lack confidence in their ability to remember things, and many also believe that it is important to remember almost everything. To avoid the possibility of forgetting information from something they read, they keep the paper or magazine instead. In addition, they want to keep important things in sight as reminders of their existence. To them, putting anything out of sight means they may not remember they have it. The sight of an object appears to increase its value such that seemingly unimportant things (e.g., scraps of paper with unrecognized phone numbers) are elevated to the same status as important things (e.g., paychecks). Because those who hoard define so many things as important, nearly everything must be left in sight. At the time a possession is being used, it has a high level of "importance" and consequently gets put on top of the pile—in sight. Subsequent items take over as "important" and go on top of the previous "important" item, burying it in the pile. The pile consists of layers of once-"important" possessions.

Another complication is a problem with evaluating the costs and benefits of saving. When trying to discard or organize, thoughts about the cost of discarding dominate the person's consideration. Little or no consideration is given to the cost of saving a possession or the benefit of getting rid of it. The same problem is evident for resisting acquiring.

Problems With Emotional Attachments to Possessions

People with compulsive hoarding demonstrate emotional attachments to possessions that are different from, or at least more extreme than, those without hoarding problems. They show excessive sentimental attachments to seemingly meaningless objects. These objects are sometimes reminders of important past events, and sometimes they are things the person feels are a part of them. Throwing them away is like losing a part of themselves. The perception that having possessions means safety and comfort is another way in which emotional overattachment is evident among those who hoard. Possessions seem to provide some sense of continuity or familiarity and, consequently, they have a comforting quality. Finally, people who hoard experience a sense of loss when discarding possessions that may be similar to the experience of losing a loved one.

Thinking Styles

Two aspects of thinking play a role in the problem of hoarding. The first of these is thinking styles and the second is specific beliefs about possessions. One is a *way* of thinking and the other is the *content* of that thinking. Regarding thinking styles, for a long time psychologists and psychiatrists have recognized that certain patterns of thinking influence how we feel about ourselves and the world. For example, Dr. David Burns (1989) described a series of common errors in reasoning that lead to emotional distress. Characteristic thinking patterns common in compulsive hoarding include

- All-or-nothing thinking

- Overgeneralization

- Jumping to conclusions

- Magnification/catastrophizing

- Discounting the positive

- Emotional reasoning

- Moral reasoning

- Double standard

- Labeling

- Underestimating yourself

- Overestimating yourself

Beliefs About Possessions

Several beliefs about the role and meaning of possessions are common among people who save compulsively. These beliefs may be important in the maintenance of the behavior.

Lost opportunities and lost information are frequent worries for people with hoarding problems. The first of these might be manifest in the belief that throwing something away will waste a valuable opportunity. The second might lead to saving old newspapers so the information contained in them is not lost.

An elaborate sense of *responsibility* for the proper use of a possession is a common response among those who hoard. That is, it is important to them that their possessions not be wasted. It is as though ownership carries with it a responsibility to see that an object is not discarded if it has some potential use, no matter how unlikely. In this sense, every possession is seen as being useful to someone. Even if those who hoard cannot see themselves needing the object in the future, they can imagine someone who may need it. Once imagined, they feel it is their responsibility to save the object for that person, even if there is no concrete plan to get the object to that person. Related to responsibility is the idea that one must not be wasteful.

Another type of belief about responsibility is to be prepared for every imaginable contingency. Imagining a situation in which the person who hoards may need a possession leads them to feel responsible for keeping the possession "just in case."

Another set of beliefs often held by people who hoard is about the *emotional comfort* value of possessions. An example of this belief is "Without my possessions, I would be vulnerable" or "Throwing this out is like throwing away part of myself."

Also, many people with a hoarding problem believe they must maintain *control* over their possessions. Consequently, they may get upset and angry if someone uses, touches, or even comes near their possessions.

Finally, connected to *confidence in memory* problems are beliefs about the need for saved items to compensate for a poor memory. For example, "If I don't have things in sight, I'll forget about them." "Even if I've read the newspaper, I must keep it, because I'll forget what I've read."

Many people who hoard are *perfectionistic;* they hold excessively high standards for themselves and behave as if perfection is possible. Taking advantage of every opportunity that presents itself and remembering everything they read are unrealistic expectations that those who hoard often hold for themselves. Saving allows them to maintain the belief that it is possible to know everything in the newspaper, for example.

Most people with this problem have a tendency to exaggerate the *importance of possessions* and/or the value of information. For example, "If a possession has any potential value, I must save it." "Each of my possessions is so unique that there is nothing else like it in the world." "If I don't collect this information now, I'll never be able to get it again." "If I can possibly imagine a use for something, then it must be important and worth saving."

Behavioral Avoidance

The result of the cognitive processing problems described earlier is avoidance behavior. There are a number of things hoarding allows the person to avoid. A careful analysis of these is crucial. Saving and putting things in a pile in the middle of the room allows the person to avoid making decisions about what to save and how to organize it. The person can also avoid emotional upset or discomfort associated with discarding a cherished possession or wasting something of value. Acquiring something they can't afford enables the person to avoid dealing with unpleasant feelings.

The intervention program described here grew out of our work with a number of clients whom we studied intensively in individual treatment and in group treatment. Their therapy consisted of clinic visits to work on reducing acquiring, and learning skills for organizing, sorting possessions, making decisions about what to get rid of, changing beliefs, and reducing avoidance of difficult emotions and tasks. Regular but less frequent home sessions enabled people to gain lasting skills in their own home situation.

During the past few years, this therapy has been tested on more than 50 clients who exhibited moderate to severe hoarding problems and who often had some other problems like attention deficit disorder (ADD), depression, marital problems, and social anxiety. Some of these clients functioned very well at work and in their social lives, but were unable to make headway with the severe clutter that filled all their living spaces and rendered the home useless for all but bathing and sleeping. Others had more problems in their work, social, and family lives, but they improved nonetheless.

We have tested the effects of the therapy described here on two groups of clients with hoarding problems. The first was an open trial for nine women who ranged in age from 25 to 70 years. All of them completed 26 sessions over a period of about nine months, with every fourth session held at home or sometimes in places where they acquired things and needed to practice resisting this. These clients showed significant reductions (25–34%) in measures of hoarding severity, and 57% of them were rated "much improved" or "very much improved."

We revised the manual based on what we learned in this study and then tested the effects of treatment in a wait list-controlled study that is ongoing. In this study we randomly assigned clients either to the treatment or to a 12-week wait list followed by the treatment. Again, treatment consisted of 26 sessions over eight or nine months, with home visits occurring every month. Of the 43 people who began the therapy program, only six (14%) did not continue for various reasons, such as deciding to work on another problem they considered more important, or the inability to find the time to devote to the treatment. These clients ranged in age from 42 to 66 years, and about 35% were men. So far, 10 people have completed the 12-week wait period. We compared their outcomes with those of 13 people who completed the first 12 weeks of the treatment program. Even after only 12 weeks, clients who received the therapy showed significantly more reduction in their hoarding symptoms (26%) compared with those on the wait list (11%). Although it may not seem like it, statistically, this difference is considered very large. After 26 sessions, the 17 patients who have completed treatment so far have experienced a 45% reduction in their hoarding symptoms—an even larger effect. These findings are very positive, especially for a problem that has not responded well to medications or to other psychotherapy methods.

Brief Description of the Program

Throughout this treatment program you will learn various skills and techniques for dealing with your compulsive hoarding and excessive acquiring. During the first few sessions with your clinician, you will assess your hoarding problem and how it affects your life. Your clinician will want to visit you in your home to get a better idea of the extent of your hoarding. You will also draw a model on paper of your hoarding behavior, which will help you to understand your symptoms better and how they developed. Later sessions focus on preparing for treatment and selecting the most effective intervention methods for your specific case. In every session, your clinician will work with you to keep you motivated.

The early part of the treatment is focused on teaching you problem-solving and decision-making skills. You'll develop a Personal Organizing Plan and put it into effect. You will be asked to participate in sorting and decision-making exercises, which will help you get used to the discomfort of making hard choices, getting rid of items, and not acquiring things if this is a problem for you. With your clinician's help, you will sort through your possessions room by room, and learn to discard, recycle, and donate the things you don't need. This work will include examining how you think about your possessions, and beliefs you hold that might or might not be true. You'll be asked to take different perspectives on your acquiring and saving preferences to help you change thinking that contributes to the clutter problem. Finally, you will learn strategies for anticipating and coping with stressors and maintaining your new habits. All this work will be done collaboratively with your clinician, who will ask you to observe closely your own thoughts, emotions, and behaviors, and will invite your views on the best ways to make the changes you need.

You will probably struggle with motivation to keep working on hoarding when you find yourself feeling anxious, guilty, or depressed. Old habits, even ones you know are bad, are hard to break. This treatment program is designed to help you do just that in a supportive relationship with your clinician, who will help you stay focused on the tasks ahead.

Using This Workbook

This workbook contains all the forms, worksheets, and exercises you need to participate in this treatment program. You will move through this book under the direction of your clinician. Each chapter includes a list of goals and is focused on specific methods or techniques to help you assess your problem, understand it, and modify your thoughts, feelings, and behaviors. Interactive forms and worksheets are included in each chapter where they are first introduced. Additional copies are included in the appendix and can also be downloaded from the Treatments *That Work*™ website at www.oup.com/us/ttw. Follow your clinician's instructions for using these forms. Homework exercises are listed at the end of each chapter and will be assigned by your clinician.

It is quite easy to misplace or lose your workbook in the clutter of your home, so it is critical that you use this workbook and refer to it regularly. You should bring it to every session and talk to your clinician about the best place to keep it.

References

Burns, D. (1989). *Feeling good handbook*. New York: Morrow.

Frost, R.O. & Steketee, G. (1998). Hoarding: Clinical aspects and treatment strategies. In M. Jenike, L. Baer, & J. Minichiello, *Obsessive Compulsive Disorder: Practical Management* (3rd Ed). St. Louis: Mosby Year Book.

Chapter 2

Assessment

Goals

- To complete various assessment measures

- To allow your clinician to visit you in your home

- To choose a family member or friend as your "coach"

During each session with your clinician, you will complete a Personal Session Form. Use this form to make notes about your agenda, points you want to recall from the session, homework assignments, and any topics you want to discuss next time. A blank form is included on page 10 and additional copies can be found in the appendix or downloaded from the Treatments *ThatWork*™ website at www.oup.com/us/ttw.

Self-Assessment

Use the Saving Inventory–Revised form, the Clutter Image Rating form, the Saving Cognitions Inventory, the Activities of Daily Living Scales, and the Obsessive-Compulsive Inventory–Revised (included on pages 11–20) to determine whether you have a problem with compulsive hoarding and to what degree it affects your life. Your clinician will work with you to score these measures and discuss the results with you.

Home Visit

At some point within the first few sessions of your treatment, your clinician will want to visit you in your home. During this visit, your clinician will work with you on sorting, organizing, and removing clutter. You will assemble a box or bag of typical saved items for use during your clinic appointments to learn and practice new skills. This box should contain random clutter from your house, such as junk mail, newspapers, magazines,

Personal Session Form

Initials: _____   Session #: _____   Date: _____

Agenda:

_____

_____

_____

Main Points:

_____

_____

_____

_____

_____

_____

Homework:

_____

_____

To discuss next time:

_____

_____

_____

_____

Intervention strategies used or reviewed:

_____

_____

_____

_____

Saving Inventory–Revised

Client initials: _____   Date: _____

For each question below, circle the number that corresponds most closely to your experience DURING THE PAST WEEK.

0----------------------1----------------------2----------------------3----------------------4

None	A little	A Moderate Amount	Most/Much	Almost All/ Complete

1. How much of the living area in your home is cluttered with possessions? (Consider the amount of clutter in your kitchen, living room, dining room, hallways, bedrooms, bathrooms, or other rooms). 0 1 2 3 4

2. How much control do you have over your urges to acquire possessions? 0 1 2 3 4

3. How much of your home does clutter prevent you from using? 0 1 2 3 4

4. How much control do you have over your urges to save possessions? 0 1 2 3 4

5. How much of your home is difficult to walk through because of clutter? 0 1 2 3 4

For each question below, circle the number that corresponds most closely to your experience DURING THE PAST WEEK.

0----------------------1----------------------2----------------------3----------------------4

Not at all	Mild	Moderate	Considerable/Severe	Extreme

6. To what extent do you have difficulty throwing things away? 0 1 2 3 4

7. How distressing do you find the task of throwing things away? 0 1 2 3 4

8. To what extent do you have so many things that your room(s) are cluttered? 0 1 2 3 4

9. How distressed or uncomfortable would you feel if you could not acquire something you wanted? 0 1 2 3 4

10. How much does clutter in your home interfere with your social, work or everyday functioning? Think about things that you don't do because of clutter. 0 1 2 3 4

11. How strong is your urge to buy or acquire free things for which you have no immediate use? 0 1 2 3 4

continued

12. To what extent does clutter in your home cause you distress?   0   1   2   3   4

13. How strong is your urge to save something you know you may never use?   0   1   2   3   4

14. How upset or distressed do you feel about your acquiring habits?   0   1   2   3   4

15. To what extent do you feel unable to control the clutter in your home?   0   1   2   3   4

16. To what extent has your saving or compulsive buying resulted in financial difficulties for you?   0   1   2   3   4

For each question below, circle the number that corresponds most closely to your experience DURING THE PAST WEEK.

0--------------------1--------------------2--------------------3--------------------4

| Never | Rarely | Sometimes/ Occasionally | Frequently/ Often | Very Often |

17. How often do you avoid trying to discard possessions because it is too stressful or time consuming?   0   1   2   3   4

18. How often do you feel compelled to acquire something you see? e.g., when shopping or offered free things?   0   1   2   3   4

19. How often do you decide to keep things you do not need and have little space for?   0   1   2   3   4

20. How frequently does clutter in your home prevent you from inviting people to visit?   0   1   2   3   4

21. How often do you actually buy (or acquire for free) things for which you have no immediate use or need?   0   1   2   3   4

22. To what extent does the clutter in your home prevent you from using parts of your home for their intended purpose? For example, cooking, using furniture, washing dishes, cleaning, etc.   0   1   2   3   4

23. How often are you unable to discard a possession you would like to get rid of?   0   1   2   3   4

See score key at end of appendix.

Clutter Image Rating

Client initials: _____   Date: _____   Therapist: _____

Using the 3 series of pictures (CIR: Living Room, CIR: Kitchen, and CIR: Bedroom), please select the picture that best represents the amount of clutter for each of the rooms of your home. Put the number on the line below.

Please pick the picture that is closest to being accurate, even if it is not exactly right.

If your home does not have one of the rooms listed, just put NA for "not applicable" on that line.

Room	Number of closest corresponding picture (1–9)
Living Room	_____
Kitchen	_____
Bedroom #1	_____
Bedroom #2	_____

Also, please rate other rooms in your house that are affected by clutter on the lines below. Use the *CIR: Living Room* pictures to make these ratings.

Dining room   _____

Hallway   _____

Garage   _____

Basement   _____

Attic   _____

Car   _____

Other   _____   Please specify: _____

Clutter Image Rating Scale: Kitchen

Please select the photo below that most accurately reflects the amount of clutter in your room.

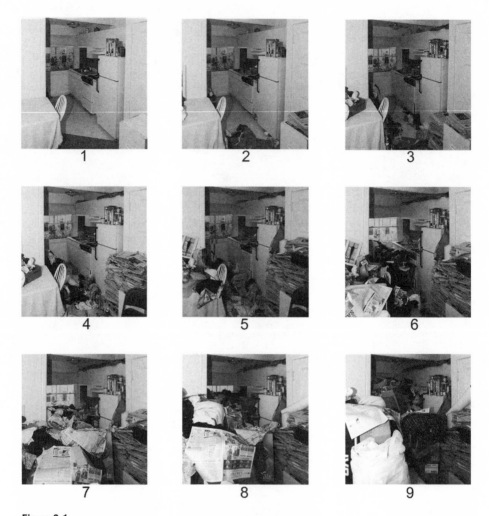

Figure 2.1

Clutter Image Rating Scale: Kitchen.

Clutter Image Rating: Living Room

Please select the photo below that most accurately reflects the amount of clutter in your room.

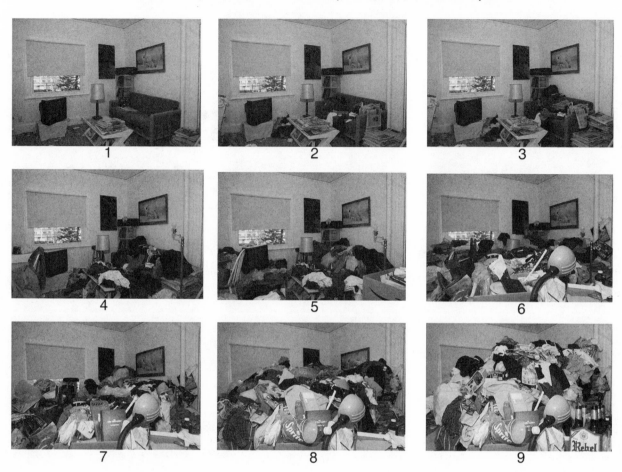

Figure 2.2

Clutter Image Rating Scale: Living Room.

continued

Clutter Image Rating: Bedroom
Please select the photo that most accurately reflects the amount of clutter in your room.

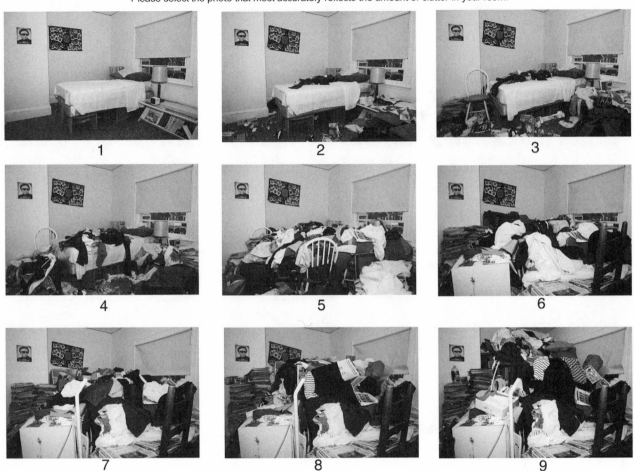

Figure 2.3

Clutter Image Rating Scale: Bedroom.

Saving Cognitions Inventory

Client initials: _____   Date: _____

Use the following scale to indicate the extent to which you had each thought when you were deciding whether to throw something away *during the past week*. If you did not try to discard anything during the past week, indicate how you would have felt if you had tried to discard something.

1----------------2----------------3----------------4----------------5---------------6--------------7

not at all   sometimes   very much

1. I could not tolerate it if I were to get rid of this.	1 2 3 4 5 6 7
2. Throwing this away means wasting a valuable opportunity.	1 2 3 4 5 6 7
3. Throwing away this possession is like throwing away a part of me.	1 2 3 4 5 6 7
4. Saving this means I don't have to rely on my memory.	1 2 3 4 5 6 7
5. It upsets me when someone throws something of mine away without my permission.	1 2 3 4 5 6 7
6. Losing this possession is like losing a friend.	1 2 3 4 5 6 7
7. If someone touches or uses this, I will lose it or lose track of it.	1 2 3 4 5 6 7
8. Throwing away some things would feel like abandoning a loved one.	1 2 3 4 5 6 7
9. Throwing this away means losing a part of my life.	1 2 3 4 5 6 7
10. I see my belongings as extensions of myself; they are part of who I am.	1 2 3 4 5 6 7
11. I am responsible for the well-being of this possession.	1 2 3 4 5 6 7
12. If this possession may be of use to someone else, I am responsible for saving it for them.	1 2 3 4 5 6 7
13. This possession is equivalent to the feelings I associate with it.	1 2 3 4 5 6 7
14. My memory is so bad I must leave this in sight or I'll forget about it.	1 2 3 4 5 6 7
15. I am responsible for finding a use for this possession.	1 2 3 4 5 6 7
16. Throwing away some things would feel like part of me is dying.	1 2 3 4 5 6 7
17. If I put this into a filing system, I'll forget about it completely.	1 2 3 4 5 6 7
18. I like to maintain sole control over my things.	1 2 3 4 5 6 7
19. I'm ashamed when I don't have something like this when I need it.	1 2 3 4 5 6 7
20. I must remember something about this, and I can't if I throw this away.	1 2 3 4 5 6 7
21. If I discard this without extracting all the important information from it, I will lose something.	1 2 3 4 5 6 7
22. This possession provides me with emotional comfort.	1 2 3 4 5 6 7
23. I love some of my belongings the way I love some people.	1 2 3 4 5 6 7
24. No one has the right to touch my possessions.	1 2 3 4 5 6 7

Activities of Daily Living Scales

Client initials: _____   Date: _____

A. Activities of Daily Living

Sometimes clutter in the home can prevent you from doing ordinary activities. For each of the following activities, please circle the number that best represents the degree of difficulty you experience in doing this activity because of the clutter or hoarding problem. If you have difficulty with the activity for other reasons (for example, unable to bend or move quickly because of physical problems), do not include this in your rating. Instead, rate only how much difficulty you would have as a result of hoarding. If the activity is not relevant to your situation (for example, you don't have laundry facilities or animals), circle NA.

Activities affected by clutter or hoarding problem	Can do it easily	Can do it with a little difficulty	Can do it with moderate difficulty	Can do it with great difficulty	Unable to do	Not Applicable
1. Prepare food	1	2	3	4	5	NA
2. Use refrigerator	1	2	3	4	5	NA
3. Use stove	1	2	3	4	5	NA
4. Use kitchen sink	1	2	3	4	5	NA
5. Eat at table	1	2	3	4	5	NA
6. Move around inside the house	1	2	3	4	5	NA
7. Exit home quickly	1	2	3	4	5	NA
8. Use toilet	1	2	3	4	5	NA
9. Use bath/shower	1	2	3	4	5	NA
10. Use bathroom sink	1	2	3	4	5	NA
11. Answer door quickly	1	2	3	4	5	NA
12. Sit in sofa/chair	1	2	3	4	5	NA
13. Sleep in bed	1	2	3	4	5	NA
14. Do laundry	1	2	3	4	5	NA
15. Find important things (such as bills, tax forms, and so forth)	1	2	3	4	5	NA
16. Care for animals	1	2	3	4	5	NA

B. Living Conditions

Please circle the number that best indicates how much of a problem you have with the following conditions in your home.

Problems in the home	None	A little	Somewhat/ moderate	Substantial	Severe
17. Structural damage (floors, walls, roof, and so on)	1	2	3	4	5
18. Presence of rotten food items	1	2	3	4	5
19. Insect infestation	1	2	3	4	5
20. Presence of human urine or feces	1	2	3	4	5
21. Presence of animal urine or feces	1	2	3	4	5
22. Water not working	1	2	3	4	5
23. Heat not working	1	2	3	4	5

C. Safety Issues

Please indicate whether you have any concerns about your home like those described in the following table.

Type of problem	Not at all	A little	Somewhat/ moderate	Substantial	Severe
24. Does any part of your house pose a fire hazard? Consider, for example, a stove covered with paper, flammable objects near the furnace, and so forth.	1	2	3	4	5
25. Are parts of your house un-sanitary? Are the bathrooms unclean? Is there a strong odor?	1	2	3	4	5
26. Would medical emergency personnel have difficulty moving equipment through your home?	1	2	3	4	5
27. Are any exits from your home blocked?	1	2	3	4	5
28. Is it unsafe to move up or down the stairs or along other walkways?	1	2	3	4	5
29. Is there clutter outside your house, such as in your porch, yard, alleyway, or common areas (if you live in an apartment or condo)?	1	2	3	4	5

Obsessive–Compulsive Inventory–Revised

Client initials: _____   Date: _____

The following statements refer to experiences that many people have in their everyday lives. Circle the number that best describes how much that experience has *distressed* or *bothered* you during the *past month* using the following scale:

0-------------------1--------------------2--------------------3--------------------4

Not at all	A little	Moderately	A lot	Extremely

1. I have saved up so many things that they get in the way.	0	1	2	3	4
2. I check things more often than necessary.	0	1	2	3	4
3. I get upset if objects are not arranged properly.	0	1	2	3	4
4. I feel compelled to count while I am doing things.	0	1	2	3	4
5. I find it difficult to touch an object when I know it has been touched by strangers or certain people.	0	1	2	3	4
6. I find it difficult to control my own thoughts.	0	1	2	3	4
7. I collect things I don't need.	0	1	2	3	4
8. I repeatedly check doors, windows, drawers, and so on.	0	1	2	3	4
9. I get upset if others change the way I have arranged things.	0	1	2	3	4
10. I feel I have to repeat certain numbers.	0	1	2	3	4
11. I sometimes have to wash or clean myself simply because I feel contaminated.	0	1	2	3	4
12. I am upset by unpleasant thoughts that come into my mind against my will.	0	1	2	3	4
13. I avoid throwing things away because I am afraid I might need them later.	0	1	2	3	4
14. I repeatedly check gas and water taps, and light switches after turning them off.	0	1	2	3	4
15. I need things to be arranged in a particular order.	0	1	2	3	4
16. I feel that there are good and bad numbers.	0	1	2	3	4
17. I wash my hands more often and longer than necessary.	0	1	2	3	4
18. I frequently get nasty thoughts and have difficulty getting rid of them.	0	1	2	3	4

small objects, receipts, notes, ticket stubs, clothing, books, and so on. These clutter items should be selected mainly from the room in which treatment will begin.

If you are living with someone who is affected by your hoarding problem, your clinician may want to meet with him or her during the home visit as well.

Picking a Coach

Some family members or friends who are especially calm, thoughtful, and empathic people can be enlisted as official coaches during the intervention. Discuss this with your clinician to determine whether anyone qualifies for this role. Your "coach" will help you and provide guidance throughout the course of your treatment. The following "Instructions for Coaches" section provides written suggestions for this purpose.

Instructions for Coaches

Overcoming compulsive hoarding is often very difficult. Many people find it extremely helpful to have a support person or "coach" who can assist them with the process. As a coach, you will work together as a team with the clinician and the person with the hoarding problem. The following list outlines some ways to make your involvement most helpful. Compulsive hoarding is not a single, simple problem. Rather, it may consist of several interconnected problems that can include

- *Excessive clutter.* This is the most easily recognized symptom of hoarding. Often, the clutter becomes so overwhelming that the person has a hard time knowing where to start.

- *Problems organizing and making decisions.* A person with a hoarding problem may have difficulty thinking clearly about their clutter or what to do about it. They may have a hard time recognizing the difference between items that are useful versus nonuseful, valuable versus nonvaluable, or sentimental versus nonsentimental. Therefore, to be on the safe side, they may treat all items as if they are useful, valuable, or sentimental. This leads to difficulty deciding when it is time to throw something out.

- *Difficulty letting go of possessions.* One of the most striking problems is difficulty letting go of and removing things—discarding, recycling, selling, and giving away items. This occurs even with items that seem to have little or no value. The amount of distress associated with removing clutter is enormous.

- *A tendency to avoid or procrastinate.* People with hoarding problems often feel very overwhelmed by the sheer volume of clutter and the difficult task of decision making. They may also feel depressed or nervous, which can add to a sense of fatigue and a tendency to avoid taking action. As a result, it is tempting to think "This is too big to tackle today; I'll do it tomorrow."

- *Difficulty resisting urges to acquire objects.* For many people with hoarding problems, the urge to acquire things can be very strong, almost irresistible. Some people may feel a need to buy things to complete a collection; others may feel a need to pick up free things.

Not everyone who hoards has all these problems. Every person and every hoarding problem are a little bit different, but all involve strong emotional reactions to possessions, thoughts and beliefs about saving things that are not always rational, and behaviors that enable the problem to persist. As part of our treatment program, the clinician has carefully reviewed these aspects of hoarding with the person you are assisting and has determined which problems are particularly troublesome. This is important, because the particular kinds of problems the person is facing guide what interventions to use.

We recommend coaches do the following:

- *Meet as a team* with the clinician and the person with the hoarding problem. Three people working together is a recipe for success, whereas three people working in different directions is unlikely to work.

- *Help the person to remain focused* on the task in front of them. People with hoarding problems often find themselves easily distracted, especially when they are trying to reduce clutter, make decisions about possessions, or resist the urge to acquire things. Often, the coach can be very helpful by politely reminding the person what they are supposed to be doing right now.

■ *Provide emotional support.* In our experience, acting like a taskmaster or drill sergeant just makes people feel nervous or angry and interferes with their ability to learn new approaches. They feel even more isolated and misunderstood, and revert to bad habits. Therefore, we suggest using a gentle touch. It's often very helpful to express empathy with statements such as, "I can see how hard this is for you" or "I understand that you have mixed feelings about whether to tackle this clutter." The person with the hoarding problem is going through some major stress and often needs a sympathetic ear or even a shoulder to cry on.

■ *Help the person make decisions but* do not *make decisions for them.* During treatment, the person with the hoarding problem is learning to develop new rules for deciding what to keep and what to remove. The coach can remind the person of these rules by asking questions, not by telling them what to do. Good questions are: "Is it useful?" "Do you need it?" "Can you do without it?" "In the long run, are you better off keeping it or letting it go?" The list of questions about possessions (see chapter 6) may prove useful for this purpose.

■ *Be a cheerleader.* Sometimes we all need an extra boost when things get difficult. Calling the person to remind them of their homework assignment, telling them you believe they can do it, and noticing and telling them when they are doing a good job are all good cheerleading strategies.

■ *Help with hauling.* Many people who hoard have accumulated so much clutter that it would take them a year or more to discard it all by themselves. This makes it easy to get discouraged, because progress is slow. Coaches are very helpful when they roll up their sleeves and help remove items from the home, provided that the person with the hoarding problem makes the decisions and remains fully in charge of the process.

■ *Accompany the person on nonacquisition trips.* For people who acquire too many things, the clinician often assigns homework, such as going to a tempting store or yard sale and not buying anything. It can be extremely helpful to have someone go with them to help them resist temptation and make the trip a success.

We have also found that even the most well-meaning coaches can make themselves less helpful by using the wrong strategies. Here are some don'ts:

- *Don't argue* with the person about what to get rid of and what to acquire. Long debates about the usefulness of an item or the need to get rid of it will only produce negative emotional reactions that don't facilitate progress. Instead, whenever you feel in conflict, take a break, relax a bit, and remind yourself how difficult this is for the client.

- *Don't take over decision making.* It would certainly be easier and quicker if coaches simply took charge, decided what should stay and what should go, and hauled the clutter out themselves, but this method doesn't teach clients how to manage their problem. The clutter will just build up again. Instead, be sure the client is in charge at all times and makes all decisions, with the coach's support and guidance.

- *Don't touch or move anything without permission.* Imagine how you would feel if a well-meaning person came into your home and handled your things without permission. Doing this can damage the trust between you and make it impossible for the person to proceed.

- *Don't tell the person how they should feel.* It can be very hard to understand why someone feels so sentimental about keeping what looks like trash to you or fearful about getting rid of something that is clearly useless, but these feelings developed for reasons even the client may not yet understand. Be as patient as you can. We know that coaching can be frustrating.

- *Don't work beyond your own tolerance level.* To be a good coach, you have to take care of yourself first and then help your friend or family member. So feel free to set limits on how long and how much work you can do on any given occasion. Pat yourself on the back for your own efforts; helping someone who hoards is very hard work.

Homework

✎ Review "What Is Hoarding?" from chapter 1.

✎ Complete the self-assessment questionnaires in this chapter.

✎ Assemble a box or bag of items to bring to office appointments for sorting.

Chapter 3

Your Hoarding Model

Goal

▪ To develop a model of your hoarding problem

Remember to use the Personal Session Form to make notes about your agenda, points you want to recall from the session, homework assignments, and any topics you want to discuss next time. Copies of the form are included in the appendix.

Building Your Hoarding Model

At this stage of your treatment, you will work with your clinician to develop two versions of your hoarding model. The first is a conceptual model that is intended for general reference during treatment to help you understand your behavior in the broad context of your life experience. The second is a behavioral analysis that is more specific and describes your individual episodes of acquiring or difficulty removing clutter. This analysis will help you understand why you behaved the way you did during the specific episode.

Many factors contribute to your hoarding, including personal and family vulnerabilities; information processing problems; thoughts, beliefs, and attachments to possessions; and emotional reactions. You will work with your clinician to complete the model pictured in figure 3.1.

Beliefs and Attachments to Possessions

Your beliefs about and attachments to your possessions are the driving force behind your compulsive hoarding. Review the Reasons for Saving list presented here and select the thoughts and beliefs you recognize in your own reasons for saving your possessions. Included in this list are beliefs

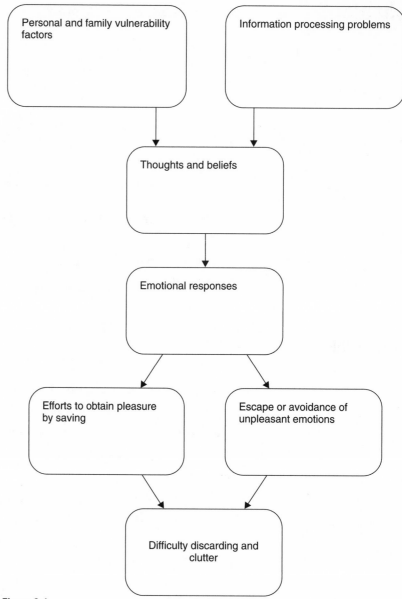

Figure 3.1

Hoarding model for _____ [client's initials].

about emotional comfort, loss and mistakes, value of possessions, identity, responsibility, memory, control, and perfectionism.

Reasons for Saving

The following types of beliefs occur commonly among people with hoarding problems:

- *Emotional comfort.* Possessions provide emotional comfort or safety and are kept to avoid anxiety or discomfort the person fears will not be tolerable. Examples include the following:

  Without this, I'll feel vulnerable.

  I can't tolerate getting rid of this.

  I feel comfortable around my stuff; I feel better.

  I sat down and built a little fortress around myself. I think I needed it.

- *Loss and mistakes.* Getting rid of possessions represents a loss of opportunity or information and seems like an irreparable mistake. The person may believe that mistakes are equivalent to failure. Examples include the following:

  Getting rid of this will mean losing information that might be important.

  Throwing something out and finding I needed it later would be a disaster.

- *Value.* Possessions have special value and need to be saved. Even unimportant things like old receipts or bottle tops seem very important. Any item that might have value must be saved, and other items cannot substitute for them. Examples include the following:

  If an object has any potential value, I must save it.

  This is so unique that there is nothing else like it in the world.

  If I can imagine a use for something, then it must be worth saving.

  If I think I might need something, it's more likely that I will really need it.

  If I don't keep/get this information now, I won't be able to get it again.

  I could only give this to a worthy person who would appreciate it properly.

- *Identity.* Possessions represent personal worth and identity. Examples include the following:

This possession represents who I am.

Part of my thing is sharing. I like to redistribute things.

Throwing away this possession is like throwing away a part of me.

Getting rid of this is sort of like burying someone.

- *Responsibility.* Having a possession carries with it a responsibility for not wasting it. "Should" statements are often associated with responsibility concerns. Examples include the following:

I'm responsible for not wasting this.

Throwing something away might be wasting a valuable opportunity.

I am responsible for finding a use for these things.

I am responsible for the well-being of my possessions.

If I have something that someone else might want, I should save it for them.

- *Memory.* Items are kept (preferably in sight) to avoid forgetting important things. People with this problem often think their memories are poor and that they need to keep objects as memory aids. Examples include the following:

Saving things means I don't have to rely on my memory.

My memory is so bad I need to keep things in sight or I'll forget about them.

If I put things into a filing system, I'll forget about them.

In my life, the past has been very important to me, so I try to hold on to it.

- *Control.* Allowing others to touch or use possessions ruins or changes them. People with this belief usually refuse to share possessions or permit others to handle them. Examples include the following:

If someone touches my things, I'll lose them or lose track of them.

People who use my things will wreck them.

When I put things away, I have the feeling I don't know where anything is.

- *Perfectionism.* Beliefs that perfection is possible and that mistakes are terrible. Examples include the following:

I have to read and understand every article before I can discard the newspaper.

I must organize everything exactly right.

Brief Thought Record

The Brief Thought Record may be helpful when working with your clinician to develop your model of hoarding and your behavioral analysis for a specific situation. Use the blank form on page 32 to record triggering events, to identify thoughts and beliefs, and to note the emotions and behaviors your thoughts and beliefs provoke. Additional copies are provided in the appendix so you can complete them as homework.

Downward Arrow Form

You may experience strong reactions during your sorting sessions with your clinician. If this occurs, use the Downward Arrow Form on page 33 to work through your emotions. Additional copies are included in the appendix.

Model of Acquiring

If you have a problem with excessive acquiring, your clinician may wish to help you develop a model that refers only to this problem. Models for acquiring have more positive feelings and fewer negative ones than models for hoarding. Use the blank hoarding model form in figure 3.1 and simply substitute the word "Acquiring" for the words "Difficulty discarding and

Brief Thought Record

Initials: _____ Date: _____

Trigger situation	Thought or belief	Emotions	Actions/behaviors

Downward Arrow Form

Item: _____

In thinking about getting rid of (discarding, recycling, selling, giving away) this, what thoughts occur to you?

_____

_____

_____

If you got rid of this, what do you think would happen?

_____

_____

_____

If this were true, why would it be so upsetting? (What would it mean to you? Why would that be so bad?)

_____

_____

_____

If that were true, what's so bad about that?

_____

_____

_____

What's the worst part about that?

_____

_____

_____

What does that mean about *you?*

_____

_____

_____

_____

Acquiring Form

Make a list of the types of items you typically bring into your home and how you acquired them. Think about items you acquired during the past week and record what items you acquire during the coming week. Do not include groceries or other perishable goods. Rate how uncomfortable you would feel if you didn't acquire this item when you saw it by using a scale of 0 to 100, where 0 equals no discomfort and 100 is the most uncomfortable you ever felt.

Item and where you typically find it	Discomfort if not acquired (0–100)

clutter." The Acquiring Form on page 34 is designed to help you become aware of every item you bring home in a week's time. Tracking this is often illuminating and will help you and your therapist develop a model for understanding the factors that drive your acquiring actions.

Homework

✎ Think about and write down the vulnerability factors (family history, experiences, strongly held beliefs) that contribute to saving and/or acquiring.

✎ Review the Reasons for Saving list presented earlier, and select thoughts and beliefs that contribute to your acquiring and saving.

✎ Complete the Acquiring Form for one week between sessions.

✎ Work on the model for hoarding and acquiring (figure 3.1) at home.

✎ Monitor your thoughts and feelings using the Brief Thought Record.

✎ Try out an experiment to discard an item or not acquire something to identify the beliefs that prompt saving and acquiring.

Chapter 4

Planning Your Treatment

Goals

▪ To establish treatment goals and set rules for treatment

▪ To complete the visualization exercises

Remember to use the Personal Session Form to make notes about your agenda, points you want to recall from the session, homework assignments, and any topics you want to discuss with your clinician during the next session. Copies of the form are included in the appendix.

Treatment Goals and Rules

At this point you will work with your clinician to establish your treatment goals and the rules you'll follow during therapy. If you have chosen someone to be your "coach," as discussed in the previous chapter, he or she should be present during this planning phase.

The Personal Goals Form on page 38 lists goals for treatment and includes a section titled "Personal Goals." Here you will identify your own goals for the coming weeks and months.

The following list of rules will ensure that your treatment progresses in a manner and at a pace you can manage. Your clinician will discuss these in further detail during the treatment planning session.

Treatment Rules

1. The clinician may not touch or remove any item without explicit permission.

2. The client makes all decisions about possessions.

3. Treatment proceeds systematically—by room, type of item, or difficulty of the task.

Goals

Treatment Goals

1. Increase my understanding of compulsive hoarding.

2. Create a usable living space.

3. Increase the appropriate use of space.

4. Improve my decision-making skills regarding my possessions.

5. Organize my possessions to make them more accessible.

6. Reduce my compulsive buying or acquisition.

7. Remove (discard, recycle, sell, give away) unneeded possessions.

8. Evaluate my beliefs about organizing, acquiring, and discarding.

9. Learn problem-solving skills.

10. Prevent future hoarding.

Personal Goals

My main goals in this treatment are

1. _____

2. _____

3. _____

4. _____

5. _____

6. _____

7. _____

8. _____

9. _____

10. _____

4. The client and clinician will establish an organizing plan before sorting possessions.

5. The client will think aloud while sorting possessions to understand and evaluate thoughts and beliefs better.

6. Only handle it once (OHIO)—or at most twice.

7. Treatment will proceed in a flexible manner.

Visualization and Practice Exercises

To understand your motivation for entering treatment for hoarding, you will complete several visualization and practice exercises. These exercises will help your clinician to plan your treatment and will also help you to clarify your thoughts and feelings about organizing, reducing clutter, and limiting acquiring.

The first exercise is to complete the Clutter Visualization Form on page 40. For this task you will visualize the current cluttered state of a specific room in your home and record your level of discomfort as you form the image in your mind. Ideally, you will choose an important room such as a kitchen, dining room, living room, or bedroom.

The second exercise is to complete the Unclutter Visualization Form on page 41. This time you will visualize the same room you did during the previous exercise, but without any clutter. Imagine that everything you want to keep is still there, but organized, sorted, and put in its proper place. How does this make you feel? Record your level of discomfort.

The third exercise is to complete the Acquiring Visualization Form on page 42.

Practice Exercises

During treatment your clinician will ask you to complete various homework assignments. One of these assignments is to perform practice exercises during which you get rid of (discard, recycle) a possession that may make you feel uncomfortable. After you have removed the item, you will record how you feel for the next few hours and days using the Practice

Clutter Visualization Form

Room: _____

A. Visualize this room with all of its present clutter. Imagine standing in the middle of the room slowly turning to see all of the clutter.

B. How uncomfortable did you feel while imagining this room with all the clutter? Use a scale from 0 to 100, where 0 = no discomfort and 100 = the most discomfort you have ever felt.

Initial Discomfort Rating: _____

C. What feelings were you having while visualizing this room?

1. _____

_____

_____

2. _____

_____

_____

3. _____

_____

_____

D. What thoughts (beliefs, attitudes) were you having while visualizing this room?

1. _____

_____

_____

2. _____

_____

_____

3. _____

_____

_____

Unclutter Visualization Form

Room: _____

A. Visualize this room with the clutter gone. Imagine cleared surfaces and floors, tabletops without piles, and uncluttered floors with only rugs and furniture. Don't think about where the things have gone; just imagine the room without clutter.

B. How uncomfortable did you feel while imagining this room without all the clutter? Use a scale from 0 to 100, where 0 = no discomfort and 100 = the most discomfort you have ever felt.

Initial Discomfort Rating: _____

C. What thoughts and feelings you were having while visualizing this room?

1. _____

   _____

   _____

2. _____

   _____

   _____

3. _____

   _____

   _____

D. Imagine what you can do in this room now that it is not cluttered. Picture how pleasant this room will feel when you have arranged it the way you want it. Describe your thoughts and feelings.

1. _____

   _____

   _____

2. _____

   _____

   _____

3. _____

   _____

   _____

E. How uncomfortable did you feel while imagining the room this way? (0 = no discomfort and 100 = the most discomfort you have ever felt)

Final Discomfort Rating: _____

Acquiring Visualization Form

Visualize a typical situation in which you have a strong urge to acquire something. In your image, don't actually pick up the item, just look at it. Please describe the location and item you imagined.

Rate how strong was your urge to acquire the item (0 = no urge to acquire, 100 = irresistible urge).

Acquiring urge _____

What thoughts did you have while you imagined this scene?

1. _____

_____

2. _____

_____

3. _____

_____

Visualize this scene again, but this time, imagine leaving without the item. How much discomfort did you experience while imagining (0 to 100).

Discomfort Rating _____

Please list any thoughts you think would help you to not acquire an object.

1. _____

_____

2. _____

_____

3. _____

_____

Now rate how uncomfortable you feel about leaving without the item(s) from 0 to 100.

Discomfort Rating _____

Practice Form

A. What was the item (to remove or not to acquire)? _____

_____

Initial discomfort (0 = no discomfort to 10 = maximal discomfort) _____

_____

_____

B. What did you do (not acquire, trash, recycle, give away, other)? _____

_____

_____

_____

Discomfort rating (0 to 10)   after 10 min   _____

after 20 min   _____

after 30 min   _____

after 40 min   _____

after 50 min   _____

after 1 hour   _____

the next day   _____

C. Conclusion regarding experiment: _____

_____

_____

_____

_____

_____

_____

Form included here. Additional copies of the form are included in the appendix.

Homework

✎ Think about your personal goals and record them on the "Personal Goals" form.

✎ Monitor your thoughts and feelings during sorting, discarding, and acquiring by completing the various visualization exercises included in this chapter.

✎ Practice getting rid of items using the Practice Form.

Chapter 5 — *Problem Solving and Organizing*

Goals

- To learn effective problem-solving skills

- To develop organizing skills

- To create and implement a Personal Organizing Plan

- To learn strategies for organizing paper and how to create a filing system

Remember to use the Personal Session Form to make notes about your agenda, points you want to recall from the session, homework assignments, and any topics you want to discuss next time. Copies of the form are included in the appendix.

Problem Solving

Learning to solve problems and to categorize, file, and store items out of sight is essential for successful resolution of hoarding. Some simple steps for problem solving are shown in table 5.1.

Problem solving is appropriate whenever you are having trouble accomplishing a task or dealing with a difficult situation. These steps may seem obvious, but it is easy to omit one or more of them and to cut a task short. Ask your therapist to help you avoid this pitfall by making sure you follow

Table 5.1 Problem-Solving Steps

1. Define the problem and contibuting factors.
2. Generate as many solutions as possible.
3. Evaluate the solutions and select one or two that seem feasible.
4. Break the solution into managable steps.
5. Implement the steps.
6. Evaluate the outcome.
7. If necessary, repeat the process until a good solution is found.

all the steps systematically, especially the step in which you generate as many solutions as possible. Be careful not to make judgments about these ideas while you generate them. This step asks you to be creative—an important key to finding good solutions.

Tracking Your Tasks

Setting priorities and keeping track of them in this workbook are the keys to maintaining your focus on treatment. We have provided you with a Task List form on page 47 to help you keep track of all your planned activities. Additional copies of this organizing tool are included in the appendix.

Your Organizing Skills

Your clinician will begin the organizing skills section of your treatment by helping your learn the best ways to organize your possessions. The first step is to define a few categories for items that will be removed from your home and then work on categorizing items that you will save.

Unwanted Items

The following categories are likely to be the main choices for how to dispose of any items you would like to remove from your home:

- Trash

- Recycle

- Donate (e.g., charities, library, friends, family)

- Sell (e.g., yard sale, bookstore, consignment shop, Internet sales)

- Undecided

You will work with your clinician to develop an action plan for how and when to remove items in each of these categories.

Task List

Priority Rating	Task	Date Put on List	Date Completed
A			
•			
•			
•			
•			
•			
•			
B			
•			
•			
•			
•			
•			
•			
C			
•			
•			
•			
•			
•			

Items to Save

The general organizing plan shown here includes a long list of categories of saved items (e.g., mail, photos, clothing, newspapers, office supplies) and typical locations where most people keep them.

Organizing Plan

Categories for Saving	Locations for Storage
1. Mail and miscellaneous paper	File cabinets, drawers, processing pile
2. Magazines	Shelves, display, storage
3. Photos	Drawers, boxes
4. Newspapers	Recycle box
5. Clothing	Drawers, closets, laundry basket
6. Coats	Closets, rack
7. Boots and shoes	Closets, shoe rack
8. Books	Shelves, storage
9. Audio and videotapes	Shelves, drawers
10. Souvenirs	Display cabinets, drawers, storage
11. Decorative items	On display, storage
12. Gifts	Storage
13. Office supplies	Desk drawer, shelf, top of desk
14. Games	Shelves, cabinets
15. Hardware	Basement, garage, kitchen drawer
16. Furniture	Placed in room, storage
17. Empty containers	Cupboards, basement, garage
18. Food	Refrigerator, cupboard, pantry
19. Kitchen utensils	Drawers, containers
20. Pots, pans, and dishes	Cupboards, on hooks

21.	Linens	Dining room cabinet, linen closet
22.	Toiletries	Bathroom shelves, cabinets, drawers
23.	Cleaning products	Kitchen, bath or laundry cabinets
24.	Cleaning tools	Closet
25.	Garden and yard tools	Garage, basement
26.	Recreation equipment	Garage, basement, attic, closet
27.	Paint and equipment	Garage, basement
28.	Pet food and equipment	Closet, cupboard
29.	Handicrafts	Cabinet, shelf, basement

The blank Personal Organizing Plan on page 50 will help you determine what kinds of items clutter your home and need to be classified and organized. From the general organizing plan, choose and list a category for each item in your home that needs to be categorized in the left-hand column of your Personal Organizing Plan and write down the final location (room, piece of furniture, and so forth) where each item belongs. You must eventually have an appropriate storage/filing location for all your things. Filing cabinets, bookshelves, and other storage furnishings may be needed to help you get organized.

The Preparing for Organizing Form on page 51 will help you decide what preparations are needed before you are able to begin major sorting tasks. Begin by selecting a room and determining what types of objects you have within that space. Think through how you would store these objects when you have finished sorting them all. Do you need bookcases, file folders, a filing cabinet, hangers for a closet, plastic bins, or any other storage strategies? Record these items on the form so you can obtain them before you start.

After the organizing plan, necessary equipment, and storage locations are in place, you can begin sorting your things using the decision tree shown in figure 5.1.

Personal Organizing Plan

Target area: _____

Item category	**Final location**
1. _____	_____
2. _____	_____
3. _____	_____
4. _____	_____
5. _____	_____
6. _____	_____
7. _____	_____
8. _____	_____
9. _____	_____
10. _____	_____
11. _____	_____
12. _____	_____
13. _____	_____
14. _____	_____
15. _____	_____
16. _____	_____
17. _____	_____
18. _____	_____
19. _____	_____
20. _____	_____

Preparing for Organizing Form

Room selection: _____

Target area or type of object selected: _____

Things I need to do to prepare for organizing:

1. _____

_____

2. _____

_____

3. _____

_____

4. _____

_____

5. _____

_____

6. _____

_____

Suggested tasks include:

- Getting boxes or storage containers

- Getting labels for boxes

- Clearing space for interim and final destinations

- Clearing space for sorting

- Scheduling times for working

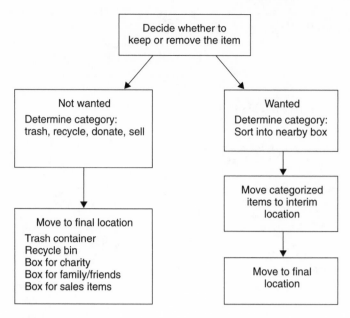

Figure 5.1

Decision tree.

Organizing and Filing Paper

People who hoard often mix important and unimportant things, such as checks and bills mixed with grocery store flyers and newspapers. To help you organize paperwork, it is crucial to set up a filing system for bills and documents, as well as places to store other papers like informational materials, upcoming events, travel information, pictures, and so on. Establishing a filing system early on helps with the sorting of items in each room. You might want to consult with friends or family members who seem to be well organized for ideas and suggestions.

Deciding how to file your paperwork can be difficult. We provide some suggestions in the following list.

How Long to Save Paper

Keep for One Month

■ Credit card receipts

- Sales receipts for minor purchases

- Withdrawal and deposit slips. Toss after you've checked them against your monthly bank statement.

Keep for One Year

- Paycheck stubs/direct deposit receipts

- Monthly bank, credit card, brokerage, mutual fund, and retirement account statements

Keep for Six Years

- W-2 forms, 1099s, and other "guts" of your tax returns

- Year-end credit card statements, and brokerage and mutual fund summaries

Keep Indefinitely

- Tax returns

- Receipts for major purchases

- Real estate and residence records

- Wills and trusts

Keep in a Safety Deposit Box

- Birth and death certificates

- Marriage licenses

- Insurance policies

Review the Filing Paper Form included on page 54 to determine which of the categories listed are relevant for your own filing system.

Like you did earlier, you may complete another Personal Organizing Plan, but this time, do it for all your paper items (see page 55). A few simple general organizing rules like those listed in figure 5.2 can be photocopied from this workbook and posted on your refrigerator door (Anne Goodwin, 2006, April, personal communication).

Filing Paper Form

- Addresses and phone numbers
- Archives: wills, insurance policies, other important papers
- Articles (unread; after reading, put in a file of their own [e.g., Garden, Cooking])
- Automobile
- Catalogs
- Checking account(s)
- Computer
- Correspondence
- Coupons
- Diskettes
- Entertainment
- Financial
  - Credit cards
  - Bank statements
  - Retirement
  - Savings account(s)
  - Stocks
- Humor
- Individuals (by name); one file for each household member
- Instruction manuals/warranties
- Medical
- Personal/sentimental
- Photographs (before they get installed in an album)
- Product information
- Restaurants
- School papers
- Services
- Stamps
- Stationery
- Taxes
- Things-to-do lists
- Things to file (things that have to be reviewed)
- Calendar items (reminders for that specific month)
- Trips/vacation information

Things I need to get for filing paper:

1. _____

_____

2. _____

_____

3. _____

_____

4. _____

Suggested items include
- File folders
- Hanging files
- Filing cabinets
- Labels
- Desk organizer

Personal Organizing Plan for Papers

Target area: _____

Item category   **Final location**

1. _____   _____

2. _____   _____

3. _____   _____

4. _____   _____

5. _____   _____

6. _____   _____

7. _____   _____

8. _____   _____

9. _____   _____

10. _____   _____

11. _____   _____

12. _____   _____

13. _____   _____

14. _____   _____

15. _____   _____

16. _____   _____

17. _____   _____

18. _____   _____

19. _____   _____

20. _____   _____

If you take it out, put it back.

If you open it, close it.

If you throw it down, pick it up.

If you take it off, hang it up.

If you use it, clean it up.

Figure 5.2
General organizing rules.

Homework

- ✎ Practice problem-solving steps for a problem identified during one of your sessions.

- ✎ Call charities and sales outlets to make plans to remove unwanted possessions.

- ✎ Fill out the Preparing for Organizing Form and complete the selected tasks before your next session.

- ✎ Complete the Personal Organizing Plan and use it to sort items in the current target work area and move them to their intended location.

- ✎ Complete an additional Personal Organizing Plan for paper items.

- ✎ Decide where to file paper items, assemble filing materials, generate file categories, and label file folders.

✎ Sort papers into files and put them away.

✎ Collect a few days worth of mail and bring it to your session to sort with your clinician.

✎ Bring to your session any items for discussion that you could not decide on or categorize at home.

✎ Continue, during your session, any other tasks begun at home.

✎ Develop a plan for using cleared spaces and for keeping them clear of new clutter.

Chapter 6   *Practicing Sorting*

Goals

- To develop an exposure hierarchy

- To participate in sorting and decision-making exercises

  Remember to use the Personal Session Form to make notes about your agenda, points you want to recall from the session, homework assignments, and any topics you want to discuss next time. Copies of the form are included in the appendix.

Habituation

The most effective way to overcome fear and discomfort is to expose yourself to situations you usually avoid because they make you feel uncomfortable. The more often you put yourself in a situation that is uncomfortable for you, the more you will get used to it, and the less discomfort you will feel. This process is called *habituation*. It is similar to the process that happens when you move to a new place near a train track or subway. At first, the sound bothers you, but after a while, you get used to it. Eventually, you hardly notice sounds that used to bother you a lot.

Some people habituate slowly, others quickly, and others have up-and-down reactions that gradually reduce over time. The habituation graph shown in figure 6.1 shows a gradual drop in discomfort as exposure to an uncomfortable situation continues.

Imagined Exposures

Before you participate in actual sorting exercises, either in your home or during an office session, your clinician may decide to start you off with imagined exposures. Prolonged imagined exposures can help you prepare

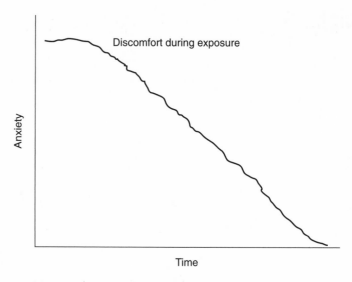

Figure 6.1
Habituation graph.

for direct exposures, especially if you are fearful of sorting and possibly discarding your possessions.

Begin by selecting a difficult situation or behavior, like letting go of something moderately difficulty—something you like, but don't love. You can use imagined exposure to challenge your beliefs as well. For instance, you can imagine losing the information in a magazine and think about why that worries you. When you have a situation in mind, try to get a vivid picture of as many details as possible, including sounds, sights, smells, touch—use all your senses. Focus on your emotional reactions to letting go as well, such as fear, guilt, or sadness. Imagine picking up the object, dropping it into the trash, and taking out the trash. Maintain the image until the emotion begins to drain away. Keep in mind that you want to imagine the worst part of the situation, the part with the most distress. Doing this actually helps you habituate faster.

Developing Your Exposure Hierarchy

Your clinician will help you develop a hierarchy of increasingly difficult sorting situations. For example, discarding papers with unidentified phone numbers may be easy for you, whereas getting rid of newspapers may be more difficult. Create your own list of items and locations in your home, ordered from easiest to hardest. Use the Exposure Hierarchy Form in-

Exposure Hierarchy Form

	Type of item	Location	Discomfort rating
1.			
2.			
3.			
4.			
5.			
6.			
7.			
8.			
9.			
10.			

cluded here. Although you will undoubtedly experience some discomfort while you sort your things, the intent is gradually to increase your tolerance for making decisions and getting rid of items.

After creating your hierarchy, you will start sorting at home and in the office. You will begin with the items that will cause the least discomfort; the "easiest" items on your list.

To help you with your sorting, review the following Questions about Possessions and select a few that seem especially useful. Ask yourself these questions for each item you sort.

- How many do I already have and is that enough?

- Do I have enough time to use, review, or read it?

- Have I used this during the past year?

- Do I have a specific plan to use this item within a reasonable time frame?

- Does this fit with my own values and needs?

- How does this compare with the things I value highly?

- Does this just seem important because I'm looking at it now?

- Is it current?

- Is it of good quality, accurate, and/or reliable?

- Is it easy to understand?

- Would I buy it again if I didn't already own it?

- Do I really need it?

- Could I get it again if I found I really needed it?

- Do I have enough space for this?

- Will not having this help me solve my hoarding problem?

Rules of Sorting

Sorting can be facilitated by creating a set of general rules that remove the necessity of making decisions about each separate object. Work with your clinician to generate rules you will find useful in determining when to discard. For example, items not used during the past year and those with more than one copy could be discarded. Another example is to get rid of all items of clothing and jewelry that are not flattering to you. It is also important to have rules for recycling, selling, and giving away items. Record your rules on the My Rules for Sorting Form included on page 63.

Clean-out

At some point you and your therapist may want to do a clean-out. Clean-outs are usually day-long affairs during which family, friends, volunteers, or cleaning crews help clear the clutter. It is best to do this after you have had some experience sorting and have developed a set of rules that seem to work well for you, enabling you to get rid of many items but save the im-

My Rules for Sorting

1. _____

2. _____

3. _____

4. _____

5. _____

portant ones. Clean-outs take careful planning, coordination, and setting of rules that everyone follows. These should be done in conjunction with your clinician. Clean-outs are a form of extended exposure.

Behavioral Experiments

Behavioral experiments provide opportunities to test some of your beliefs about possessions and how letting go of them actually affects you. They begin with a brief description of the experiment, followed by what you predict will happen. The prediction is usually your reason for saving the item. For example, "I won't be able to stand it if I throw this magazine away." Next you rate how strongly you believe the prediction and you give your initial discomfort rating. At this point, you will do the experiment (e.g., throw the object into the trash) and then record what actually happened, including your experience, a rating of your discomfort, and your observations of whether your predictions came true. The conclusions you drew from the experiment form the final part of the experiment. A blank Behavioral Experiment Form is included on page 64. Additional copies are included in the appendix.

Behavioral Experiment Form

Initials: _____   Date: _____

1. Behavioral experiment to be completed: _____
   _____
   _____

2. What do you predict (are afraid) will happen? _____
   _____
   _____
   _____

3. How strongly do you believe this will happen (0–100%) _____
   _____

4. Initial discomfort (0–10) _____

5. What actually happened? _____
   _____
   _____
   _____
   _____

6. Final discomfort (0–10) _____

7. Did your predictions come true? _____

8. What conclusions do you draw from this experiment? _____
   _____
   _____
   _____
   _____

- Imagine getting rid of items before actually discarding/recycling them.

- List items to be saved if your home would be demolished by an imminent disaster.

- Sort objects of increasingly greater difficulty and monitor your level of discomfort.

- Conduct behavioral experiments to test hypotheses, especially about discomfort and consequences of letting go of possessions.

- Take home items sorted in the clinic and store them where they belong.

- Bring in items (e.g., photos, mail, items from a particular area) to office sessions for sorting and decision-making exposures.

- Make arrangements for trash removal. In the case of a major cleanout, arrange for dumpster delivery and removal or other method for removing items.

Chapter 7

Changing Beliefs: Thinking Your Way Out of the Hoarding Box

Goals

■ To work with your clinician to identify errors in your thinking

■ To learn techniques to change beliefs and use them during your sorting sessions

Remember to use the Personal Session Form to make notes about your agenda, points you want to recall from the session, homework assignments, and any topics you want to discuss next time. Copies of the form are included in the appendix.

Errors in Thinking

Observing the ways that your thoughts contribute to your hoarding problem is one of the easiest strategies to apply during sorting sessions. Identifying patterns in your thinking helps you learn to avoid mental traps that are caused by your erroneous thoughts. The Problematic Thinking Styles list shown here will help you identify thinking errors when they occur during your office visits, as well as when completing your homework assignments.

Problematic Thinking Styles

1. *All-or-nothing thinking*—Black-or-white thinking that does not allow for shades of gray (moderation). It is exemplified by extreme words like *most, everything*, and *nothing*, and often accompanies perfectionistic standards.

   "If I can't figure out the perfect place to put this, I should just leave it here."

   "This must stay in sight or I'll forget it."

   "This is the most beautiful teapot I have ever seen and I must have it."

"I won't remember anything about this if I can't bring home this reminder."

"I'll never have another opportunity if I don't get this now."

"I can't get rid of this until I read and remember everything in this newspaper."

"Now I will forget everything I know about this subject."

2. *Overgeneralization*—Generalization from a single event to all situations by using words such as *always* or *never*

"I will never find this if I move it."

"Whenever I see a bargain, I should take advantage of it because I have always regretted not getting those pink shoes I wanted when I was 12."

"They'll think I'm a fool for passing this up."

"If I don't get it now, I'll find out later that I really needed it."

"This might be useful, so I better get it because it could be really important."

"I'll need something just as soon as I don't have it anymore."

3. *Jumping to conclusions*—Negative interpretations (e.g., predicting that things will turn out badly) without facts to support them

"If I file this magazine article, I will never be able to find it."

"I won't remember this if I move it."

"I better get this because as soon as I don't, I'll wish I had."

"My sister has offered to help me straighten up but that's because she thinks I am a terrible person and she plans to throw away everything I own."

"If I throw away this magazine, I'll soon find that I need for it."

"I must keep this newspaper because it has some useful information I am certain to need eventually."

4. *Catastrophizing*—Exaggerating the importance of an item and minimizing capabilities for obtaining needed information

    "If I put this away and can't remember where I put it, it will be awful."

    "If I don't have this information when I need it, that's when I'll find out it could have saved my husband's life."

    "I'll fall apart if I don't have this."

    "If I don't buy it now, I'll regret it forever."

    "If I throw it away, I'll go crazy thinking about it."

    "I'll never forgive myself."

5. *Discounting the positive*—Thinking that positive experiences don't count

    "Creating a filing system doesn't count as progress because there is so much more to do."

    "Resisting the urge to pick up literature at a conference doesn't count because this was minor compared with the need to spend less money buying things."

    "I didn't do a good enough job on this; others could have done it better."

    "I got this cleared, but it hardly matters because the other rooms are still cluttered."

6. *Emotional reasoning*—Allowing emotions to determine logical reasoning; confusing facts with feelings

    "It feels uncomfortable to put this out of sight, so I'll just leave it here."

    "It bothers me to leave this without getting it, so I must need it."

    "I don't want to disappoint the salesman, so I'm sure I'll find I need this."

    "If I feel uncomfortable about throwing this away, this means I should keep it."

"It seems like there must be something important in this paper. I better keep it."

7. *Moral reasoning*—"Should" statements, including "musts," "oughts," and "have to's," accompanied by guilt and frustration. Perfectionistic standards often play a role here.

"I really should be able to find any information I need at any time."

"I really should have the most up-to-date information about health problems in case something happens."

"My home should be very neat and tidy, just like other people's homes."

"I really should file this stuff."

8. *Labeling*—Attaching a negative label to oneself or others; also an extreme form of all-or-nothing thinking

"I can't find my electric bill. I'm an idiot."

"I'd feel stupid if I didn't have the right information in case someone needed it."

"I'm an idiot; I should have got that when it was cheaper."

"I can't remember what I read last week. I'm so stupid."

"I'm a loser."

"I'm a fool."

"I'm a failure."

"She's just greedy and wants all my stuff."

"He's an idiot."

9. *Underestimating oneself*—Underestimating personal ability to cope with adversity and stress

"I'll never be able to organize all this."

"If I don't get this, I won't be able to handle it and I'll have to come back for it later."

"If I do get rid of this, I won't be able to handle it."

10. *Overestimating oneself*—Assuming greater capability to accomplish a task than is reasonable

"I'll be able to organize my house home during my (week-long) vacation."

"I'll be able to resist picking up all that free literature, so I'll just go check it out."

"I'll be able to read all those newspapers eventually."

Cognitive Strategies

An important goal of this treatment program is to help you learn how to observe your own reactions and become aware of your thinking. After you and your clinician have identified the beliefs that maintain your hoarding problem, you will begin using the following cognitive strategies to change these beliefs.

Questions About Possessions

One way to help fix your errors in thinking is to pay attention to the reasons for *not* keeping an item. Review the list of Questions about Possessions from chapter 6 to determine which questions seem most useful.

Advantages and Disadvantages

Another strategy is to examine the advantages and disadvantages of keeping a particular item. People who hoard tend to focus on the immediate costs associated with discarding something, while ignoring the costs of saving all their possessions and the benefits of getting rid of them. Use the Advantages/Disadvantages Worksheet included on page 72 to help you determine the personal advantages of keeping an item, followed by the disadvantages.

Advantages/Disadvantages Worksheet

Specify the item(s) under consideration: _____

Advantages (Benefits)	Disadvantages (Costs)
Of keeping/acquiring:	Of keeping/acquiring:
Of getting rid of item:	Of getting rid of item:

Downward Arrow Method

The downward arrow method, as discussed in chapter 3, is a cognitive technique that helps clarify thoughts and beliefs. Select an item that would provoke moderate discomfort when you think about discarding it and list this on the Downward Arrow Form included on page 74.

Thought Records

During your exposure exercises, you will work to change your beliefs gradually by identifying alternative possibilities that make more sense. You will record these alternatives on the Thought Record included on page 75. Additional copies can be found in the appendix.

Defining Need Versus Want

Deciding the *true* value of a possession based on your own goals and rational thinking requires you to distinguish what you truly need from what you merely want. The Need versus Want Scale shown on pages 76–77 is useful for this purpose.

Select a current possession that would be moderately difficult but potentially appropriate for you to discard. Using the scales, record an initial rating of need and want for the particular item. Then, review the questions with your clinician to determine whether you change your ratings after thinking through the true value of possessions in relation to other important goals in your life.

Perfectionism Scale

If you are overly concerned with making mistakes, or your self-worth depends on how well you do things, it will be helpful for you to look at just how much of your life is driven by perfectionism. Use the Perfection Scale on page 78 to rate your discarding behaviors. But first, consider the following questions:

■ Do your decisions have to be perfect?

■ Do you have to get rid of things "just the right way?"

■ Do you feel defective or bad when you make mistakes in discarding?

Try to rate each of your "letting go" or sorting decisions using the Perfection Scale.

Downward Arrow Form

Item: _____

In thinking about getting rid of (discarding, recycling, selling, giving away) this, what thoughts occur to you?

_____

_____

_____

If you got rid of this, what do you think would happen?

_____

_____

_____

If this were true, why would it be so upsetting? (What would it mean to you? Why would that be so bad?)

_____

_____

_____

If that were true, what's so bad about that?

_____

_____

_____

What's the worst part about that?

_____

_____

_____

What does that mean about *you?*

_____

_____

_____

_____

Thought Record

Initials: _____   Date: _____

Trigger item or question	Automatic thought or belief	Emotions	Rational alternative (note and cognitive errors)	Outcome

Need versus Want Scales

Item being considered: _____

Rate your need for the item on the following scale below:

Need to Acquire Scale

0 ------- 1 ------- 2 ------- 3 ------- 4 ------- 5 ------- 6 ------- 7 ------- 8 ------- 9 ------- 10

No need   Required
                                                  to survive

Rate how much you want or desire the item on this scale by circling a number on the Want to Acquire Scale.

Want to Acquire Scale

0 ------- 1 ------- 2 ------- 3 ------- 4 ------- 5 ------- 6 ------- 7 ------- 8 ------- 9 ------- 10

Don't want   Desperate for

Now, let's consider the value of the item more carefully. To evaluate your true *need* for it, consider whether you need it for survival, safety, health, work, financial affairs, and/or recreation using the following questions:

- Would you die without it? _____

- Would your safety be impaired without it? _____

- Would your health be jeopardized without it? _____

- Is this critical to your work or employment? _____

- Is it essential for your financial records (e.g., tax or insurance records)? _____

Rerate your need for the item using the following Need to Acquire Scale:

Need to Acquire Scale

0 ------- 1 ------- 2 ------- 3 ------- 4 ------- 5 ------- 6 ------- 7 ------- 8 ------- 9 ------- 10

No need   Required
                                                  to survive

Need is different from want. To determine your *want* or wish for the item, think only about your urge to have it, regardless of actual need. Consider the following questions:

- Do you keep this because you like it? How much do you actually look at it?

_____

_____

_____

- Are you keeping it for sentimental reasons? Is this the best way to remember?

_____

_____

_____

- How much do you actually use it now? If you plan to use it soon, would you bet money on this?

_____

_____

_____

- Do you keep this for emotional comfort or vulnerability? Does it really protect you?

_____

_____

_____

- Does it offer information or opportunity? How real and important is that?

_____

_____

_____

Now, rerate how much you want or desire the item using the following Want to Acquire Scale:

Want to Acquire Scale

0 ------- 1 ------- 2 ------- 3 ------- 4 ------- 5 ------- 6 ------- 7 ------- 8 ------- 9 ------- 10

Don't want   Desperate for

Comments and conclusions: _____

_____

_____

_____

_____

_____

Perfection Scale

0 ---------- 1 ---------- 2 ---------- 3 ---------- 4 ---------- 5 ---------- 6 ---------- 7 ---------- 8 ---------- 9 ---------- 10

Defective   Average   Perfect

Wrong   Okay   Exactly right

Valuing Your Time

Are you saving things until you have more time to deal with them? If so, ask yourself some pointed questions:

1. Do you have more reading material (e.g., newspapers, magazines) than you can possibly read?

   ▪ If so, do you really want to spend the time necessary to read them?

   ▪ What other parts of your life will you miss or will suffer by doing so?

   ▪ How does this fit with your values and goals?

2. Do you have more _____ (fill in the blank) than you can possibly use?

   ▪ If so, do you really want to spend the time necessary to deal with them?

   ▪ What other parts of your life will you miss or will suffer by doing so?

   ▪ How does this fit with your values and goals?

Homework

✎ Review the list of Problematic Thinking Styles to identify ones that are a problem for you and develop some alternative thinking approaches.

✎ Use the Questions about Possessions (chapter 6) while sorting.

✎ Use the Advantages/Disadvantages Worksheet to decide whether to keep or get rid of items that are especially difficult for you to decide.

✎ Use the Downward Arrow Form to help you figure out why you might be having great difficulty deciding to get rid of something you know you don't really need.

✎ Use the Thought Record to identify and evaluate the accuracy of your beliefs about your possessions and to help you consider alternative beliefs.

✎ Use the Need to Acquire versus Want to Acquire scales during sorting at home when decision making seems difficult.

✎ Use the Perfection Scale during sorting at home to identify perfectionistic beliefs.

✎ Answer the valuing time questions for items that you tend to save a lot of.

✎ Practice other cognitive strategies you have learned from your clinician.

Chapter 8   *Reducing Acquiring*

Goals

- ▣ To develop rules for acquiring

- ▣ To develop an exposure hierarchy to practice reducing acquiring

- ▣ To identify and engage in pleasurable, alternative nonacquiring activities

- ▣ To learn techniques to change beliefs and use them during practice in not acquiring

Remember to use the Personal Session Form to make notes about your agenda, points you want to recall from the session, homework assignments, and any topics you want to discuss next time. Copies of the form are included in the appendix.

Excessive Acquiring

Most individuals who suffer from hoarding problems also have difficulty with excessive acquiring, either because they are compulsive buyers or because they can't say no when offered things for free. Your clinician will help you review your model of acquiring behaviors to help you understand how your behavior is triggered and reinforced. You and your clinician will work in a stepwise fashion to build your resistance to urges to acquire and to develop alternative pleasurable activities.

Establish Rules for Acquiring

If you and your clinician determine that you need to acquire fewer things, it will be helpful for you to establish rules to accomplish this goal. Work with your clinician to generate rules that help you decide when to refrain from acquiring. For example, you may decide not to acquire unless you

My Rules for Acquiring Form

1. _____

2. _____

3. _____

4. _____

5. _____

plan to use the item in the next month, or if you have an uncluttered place in your home to put the item. Record your rules on the My Rules for Acquiring worksheet included above.

Avoiding Acquiring Situations Until You Are Ready

Work with your clinician to decide how to avoid situations in which you have strong urges to acquire that you are not yet prepared to manage. For example, if you have trouble resisting yard sale items, you can decide to plan other events for Saturdays when these usually happen until you are ready to face this situation. If you can't resist special sales, you might decide not to look at the newspaper ads for a few weeks to help you avoid the problem until you are prepared to handle it using the strategies in the following paragraphs.

Advantages and Disadvantages

As you learned from chapter 7, another way to change beliefs about acquiring is to consider the advantages and disadvantages of acquiring something. People who acquire too many items often think about the immediate benefits of getting a new thing and forget about the costs of doing this. Use the Advantages/Disadvantages Worksheet for Acquiring on page 83 to help you think more clearly about whether you truly want to acquire an item. This worksheet has only two sections to help you think about the

Advantages/Disadvantages Worksheet

Specify the item(s) under consideration: _____

Advantages (Benefits) of Acquiring	Disadvantages (Costs) of Acquiring

advantages and disadvantages of acquiring something you don't yet own. Your clinician can help you decide when to use this worksheet.

Developing Your Exposure Hierarchy for Nonacquiring

Your clinician will help you develop a hierarchy of increasingly difficult situations in which you would normally acquire more items than you need. For example, driving by and standing outside shops may be relatively easy for you to accomplish alone or with others, but actually going into shops without purchasing anything is likely to be harder. Create your own list of situations, ordered from easiest to hardest using the Practice Exposure Hierarchy for Nonacquiring form included on page 85. After your hierarchy is developed, you will work with your clinician to decide which exposures you can do alone and which should be done with the help of a coach. To arrange nonshopping with a partner, work with your clinician to identify a willing and helpful family member or friend.

During your nonacquiring exposures, record your discomfort level using a scale of 0 to 10 (where 0 equals no discomfort and 10 equals the most discomfort you've ever felt) about every 10 minutes, or whenever you notice a change in discomfort. This can be done on a small card carried in your hand or by telling your coach or partner.

Alternative Sources of Enjoyment and Coping

If shopping or acquiring has become your main source of enjoyment, it is important to find replacement activities that you find equally enjoyable and fulfilling. For example, what would you like to do instead of going to flea markets or yard sales on Saturday? Use your problem-solving skills to brainstorm a short list of likely alternatives, especially those that can be done spontaneously, alone and/or in the company of friends, and inside and/or out of your home. Create your own list of alternative activities using the My Pleasurable Alternative Activities form included on page 86. List the activity and rate how pleasurable you expect it to be using a scale from 0 to 10.

Practice Exposure Hierarchy for Nonacquiring

	Situation	Discomfort rating
1.		
2.		
3.		
4.		
5.		
6.		
7.		
8.		
9.		
10.		

My Pleasurable Alternative Activities

Activity	Pleasure Rating

As for work on sorting clutter, cognitive strategies provide excellent methods for changing thinking and beliefs, and helping you cope effectively with nonacquiring exposures. The following methods are designed specifically to help you resist urges to acquire. Be sure to use them during office sessions while planning nonacquiring exposures as well as during the actual acquiring situation.

Faulty Thinking Styles

Refer to the list of Problematic Thinking Styles (chapter 7) to determine whether any of them apply to you. If so, mark them clearly so you and your clinician can notice them when they actually occur during your practice sessions.

Downward Arrow Method

The downward arrow method, as discussed in chapter 3, is a cognitive technique that helps clarify thoughts and beliefs. Select an item that would provoke moderate discomfort when you think about not acquiring it and list it on the Downward Arrow form included on page 88. How distressed, on a scale of 0 to 10, do you feel about not acquiring this item?

Defining Need Versus Want

As you did for sorting in the previous chapter, follow the steps for evaluating need versus want. Select an item you are considering acquiring and rate your need for it on a scale from 0 (don't need it at all) to 10 (need it very much) by circling the appropriate number on the scale.

Need to Acquire Scale

0 -------- 1 -------- 2 -------- 3 -------- 4 -------- 5 -------- 6 -------- 7 -------- 8 -------- 9 -------- 10

Not needed
(for survival)

Required
(for survival)

Downward Arrow Form

Item: _____

In thinking about getting rid of (discarding, recycling, selling, giving away) this, what thoughts occur to you?

_____

_____

_____

If you got rid of this, what do you think would happen?

_____

_____

_____

If this were true, why would it be so upsetting? (What would it mean to you? Why would that be so bad?)

_____

_____

_____

If that were true, what's so bad about that?

_____

_____

_____

What's the worst part about that?

_____

_____

_____

What does that mean about *you?*

_____

_____

_____

_____

Next, rate how much you want to acquire the item on the following scale by circling the appropriate number on the scale.

Want to Acquire Scale

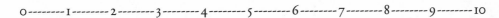

0--------1--------2--------3--------4--------5--------6--------7--------8--------9--------10

Don't want   Desperate for

If you rate your need for the item as fairly low (<5), but your rating of want for the item as moderately high (>5), you are probably experiencing a conflict between your want and your actual need. The following questions can help you reduce your wish to acquire the items. Ask yourself the following questions and then reevaluate your desire for the item:

- How much do you need to get this item?

- Would you die without it?

- Would your safety be impaired without it?

- Would your health be jeopardized?

- Must you have this for your work?

- Do you need it for financial purposes (e.g., tax or insurance records)?

- Is there some other reason why you need the item?

- Do you actually *need* this or would it just be *convenient* to have it?

Questions for Acquiring

In addition to the questions just listed about need and want, some additional questions may be useful in evaluating your urges to acquire items during exposures in stores or other locations:

- Does it fit with my own personal values and needs?

- Do I already own something similar?

- Am I only buying this because I feel bad (angry, depressed, and so on) right now?

- In a week, will I regret getting this?

- Could I manage without it?

■ If it needs fixing, do I have enough time to fix it or is my time better spent on other activities?

■ Will I actually use this item in the near future?

■ Do I have a specific place to put this?

■ Is this truly valuable or useful, or does it just seem so because I'm looking at it now?

■ Is it good quality (accurate, reliable, attractive)?

■ Will not getting this help me solve my hoarding problem?

Homework

✎ After reviewing your model for acquiring, observe how any acquiring you do during the week fits the model.

✎ Develop a list of potential exposure situations using the Exposure Hierarchy Form included in this chapter.

✎ Practice not acquiring in situations recommended by your clinician before the next session. Use a Practice Form (see appendix) for each practice situation and record your experience on this form for discussion during your next session.

✎ Practice applying your new rules for acquiring.

✎ Examine the advantages and disadvantages of acquiring an object before you make the decision.

✎ Observe any problematic thinking styles that occur when you are considering acquiring a new thing.

✎ Carefully consider how much you actually need, rather than merely want, an item you are considering acquiring.

✎ Use the list of questions about possessions while practicing not acquiring.

✎ Select and plan alternative, pleasurable activities to replace acquiring, and record how much pleasure you experienced while doing these activities.

Chapter 9   *Preventing Relapse*

Goals

■ To review your progress up to this point

■ To work with your clinician to develop strategies to continue working on your hoarding problem

■ To identify the treatment methods that worked best for you

■ To anticipate and develop strategies for coping with setbacks and lapses

Remember to use the Personal Session Form to make notes about your agenda, points you want to recall from the session, homework assignments, and any topics you want to discuss next time. Copies of the form are included in the appendix.

Reviewing Your Progress

During your final sessions with your clinician, you will review your progress up to this point and discuss how to plan for your future. You may not yet have completely achieved your goal of freedom from compulsive hoarding problems, but if you have made some progress, it is very likely that you can continue to do so. Nonetheless, changing habits takes time and you will need to work on the remaining clutter in your home and your urges to acquire for some time to come until your new habits become second nature.

Measuring Your Progress

At this stage of your treatment, your clinician will ask you to complete the assessment forms from chapter 2. These include the Saving Inventory–Revised, Clutter Image Rating form, Saving Cognitions Inventory, and Activities of Daily Living (ADL) Scales (see pages 92–100). Completing

Saving Inventory–Revised

Client initials: _____ Date: _____

For each question below, circle the number that corresponds most closely to your experience DURING THE PAST WEEK.

0---------------------1--------------------- 2 ---------------------3---------------------4

None	A little	A Moderate Amount	Most/Much	Almost All/ Complete

1. How much of the living area in your home is cluttered with possessions? (Consider the amount of clutter in your kitchen, living room, dining room, hallways, bedrooms, bathrooms, or other rooms).　　0　1　2　3　4

2. How much control do you have over your urges to acquire possessions?　　0　1　2　3　4

3. How much of your home does clutter prevent you from using?　　0　1　2　3　4

4. How much control do you have over your urges to save possessions?　　0　1　2　3　4

5. How much of your home is difficult to walk through because of clutter?　　0　1　2　3　4

For each question below, circle the number that corresponds most closely to your experience DURING THE PAST WEEK.

0---------------------1--------------------- 2 ---------------------3---------------------4

Not at all	Mild	Moderate	Considerable/Severe	Extreme

6. To what extent do you have difficulty throwing things away?　　0　1　2　3　4

7. How distressing do you find the task of throwing things away?　　0　1　2　3　4

8. To what extent do you have so many things that your room(s) are cluttered?　　0　1　2　3　4

9. How distressed or uncomfortable would you feel if you could not acquire something you wanted?　　0　1　2　3　4

10. How much does clutter in your home interfere with your social, work or everyday functioning? Think about things that you don't do because of clutter.　　0　1　2　3　4

11. How strong is your urge to buy or acquire free things for which you have no immediate use?　　0　1　2　3　4

12. To what extent does clutter in your home cause you distress? 0 1 2 3 4

13. How strong is your urge to save something you know you may never use? 0 1 2 3 4

14. How upset or distressed do you feel about your acquiring habits? 0 1 2 3 4

15. To what extent do you feel unable to control the clutter in your home? 0 1 2 3 4

16. To what extent has your saving or compulsive buying resulted in financial difficulties for you? 0 1 2 3 4

For each question below, circle the number that corresponds most closely to your experience DURING THE PAST WEEK.

0-------------------1--------------------- 2 ---------------------3--------------------4

Never	Rarely	Sometimes/ Occasionally	Frequently/ Often	Very Often

17. How often do you avoid trying to discard possessions because it is too stressful or time consuming? 0 1 2 3 4

18. How often do you feel compelled to acquire something you see? e.g., when shopping or offered free things? 0 1 2 3 4

19. How often do you decide to keep things you do not need and have little space for? 0 1 2 3 4

20. How frequently does clutter in your home prevent you from inviting people to visit? 0 1 2 3 4

21. How often do you actually buy (or acquire for free) things for which you have no immediate use or need? 0 1 2 3 4

22. To what extent does the clutter in your home prevent you from using parts of your home for their intended purpose? For example, cooking, using furniture, washing dishes, cleaning, etc. 0 1 2 3 4

23. How often are you unable to discard a possession you would like to get rid of? 0 1 2 3 4

See score key at end of appendix.

Clutter Image Rating

Client initials: _____ Date: _____

Using the three series of pictures presented at the end of this form (for the living room, kitchen, and bedroom), please select the picture that best represents the amount of clutter for each of the rooms of your home. Please pick the picture that is closest to being accurate, even if it is not exactly right, and put the number of that picture on the line next to the type of room. If your home does not have one of the rooms listed, just put NA for "not applicable" on the line next to the type of room.

Room	Number of closest corresponding picture (1–9)
Living Room	_____
Kitchen	_____
Bedroom #1	_____
Bedroom #2	_____

Also, please rate other rooms in your house that are affected by clutter on the lines below. Use the CIR: Living Room pictures to make these ratings.

Dining room	_____
Hallway	_____
Garage	_____
Basement	_____
Attic	_____
Car	_____
Other	_____

Please specify other: _____

Clutter Image Rating Scale: Kitchen

Please select the photo below that most accurately reflects the amount of clutter in your room.

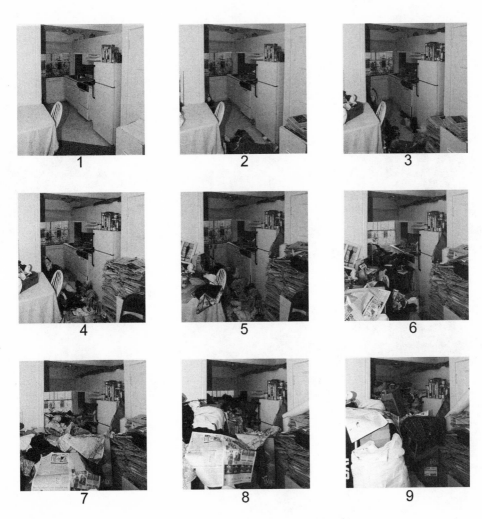

Figure 9.1

Clutter Image Rating Scale: Kitchen.

continued

Clutter Image Rating: Living Room

Please select the photo below that most accurately reflects the amount of clutter in your room.

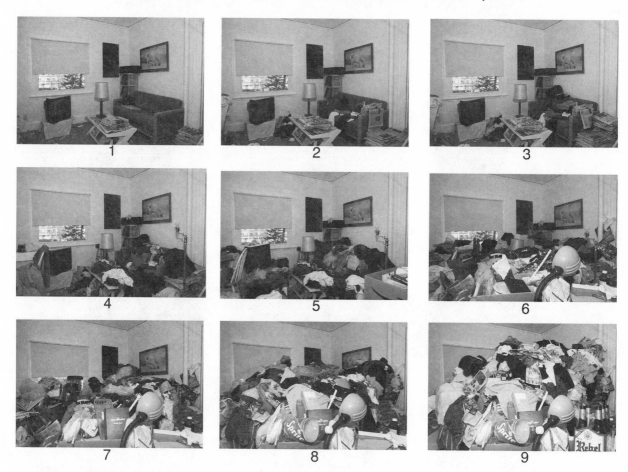

Figure 9.2

Clutter Image Rating Scale: Living Room.

Clutter Image Rating: Bedroom
Please select the photo that most accurately reflects the amount of clutter in your room.

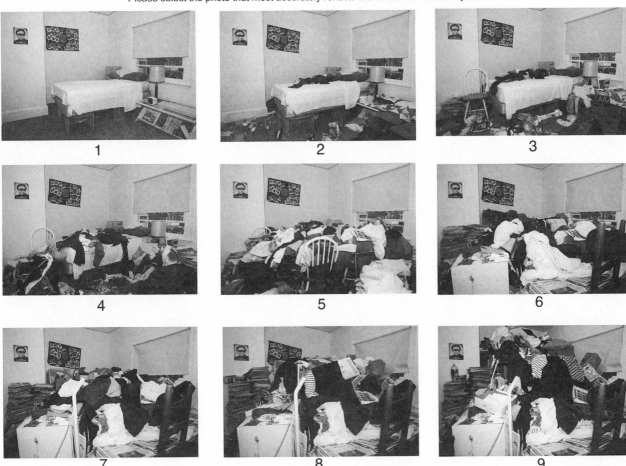

Figure 9.3

Clutter Image Rating Scale: Bedroom.

Saving Cognitions Inventory

Client initials: _____ Date: _____

Use the following scale to indicate the extent to which you had each thought when you were deciding whether to throw something away *during the past week*. If you did not try to discard anything during the past week, indicate how you would have felt if you had tried to discard something.

1---------------2---------------3---------------4---------------5---------------6---------------7

not at all   sometimes   very much

1. I could not tolerate it if I were to get rid of this.	1 2 3 4 5 6 7
2. Throwing this away means wasting a valuable opportunity.	1 2 3 4 5 6 7
3. Throwing away this possession is like throwing away a part of me.	1 2 3 4 5 6 7
4. Saving this means I don't have to rely on my memory.	1 2 3 4 5 6 7
5. It upsets me when someone throws something of mine away without my permission.	1 2 3 4 5 6 7
6. Losing this possession is like losing a friend.	1 2 3 4 5 6 7
7. If someone touches or uses this, I will lose it or lose track of it.	1 2 3 4 5 6 7
8. Throwing away some things would feel like abandoning a loved one.	1 2 3 4 5 6 7
9. Throwing this away means losing a part of my life.	1 2 3 4 5 6 7
10. I see my belongings as extensions of myself; they are part of who I am.	1 2 3 4 5 6 7
11. I am responsible for the well-being of this possession.	1 2 3 4 5 6 7
12. If this possession may be of use to someone else, I am responsible for saving it for them.	1 2 3 4 5 6 7
13. This possession is equivalent to the feelings I associate with it.	1 2 3 4 5 6 7
14. My memory is so bad I must leave this in sight or I'll forget about it.	1 2 3 4 5 6 7
15. I am responsible for finding a use for this possession.	1 2 3 4 5 6 7
16. Throwing away some things would feel like part of me is dying.	1 2 3 4 5 6 7
17. If I put this into a filing system, I'll forget about it completely.	1 2 3 4 5 6 7
18. I like to maintain sole control over my things.	1 2 3 4 5 6 7
19. I'm ashamed when I don't have something like this when I need it.	1 2 3 4 5 6 7
20. I must remember something about this, and I can't if I throw this away.	1 2 3 4 5 6 7
21. If I discard this without extracting all the important information from it, I will lose something.	1 2 3 4 5 6 7
22. This possession provides me with emotional comfort.	1 2 3 4 5 6 7
23. I love some of my belongings the way I love some people.	1 2 3 4 5 6 7
24. No one has the right to touch my possessions.	1 2 3 4 5 6 7

Activities of Daily Living Scales

Client initials: _____ Date: _____

A. Activities of Daily Living

Sometimes clutter in the home can prevent you from doing ordinary activities. For each of the following activities, please circle the number that best represents the degree of difficulty you experience in doing this activity because of the clutter or hoarding problem. If you have difficulty with the activity for other reasons (for example, unable to bend or move quickly because of physical problems), do not include this in your rating. Instead, rate only how much difficulty you would have as a result of hoarding. If the activity is not relevant to your situation (for example, you don't have laundry facilities or animals), circle NA.

Activities affected by clutter or hoarding problem	Can do it easily	Can do it with a little difficulty	Can do it with moderate difficulty	Can do it with great difficulty	Unable to do	Not Applicable
1. Prepare food	1	2	3	4	5	NA
2. Use refrigerator	1	2	3	4	5	NA
3. Use stove	1	2	3	4	5	NA
4. Use kitchen sink	1	2	3	4	5	NA
5. Eat at table	1	2	3	4	5	NA
6. Move around inside the house	1	2	3	4	5	NA
7. Exit home quickly	1	2	3	4	5	NA
8. Use toilet	1	2	3	4	5	NA
9. Use bath/shower	1	2	3	4	5	NA
10. Use bathroom sink	1	2	3	4	5	NA
11. Answer door quickly	1	2	3	4	5	NA
12. Sit in sofa/chair	1	2	3	4	5	NA
13. Sleep in bed	1	2	3	4	5	NA
14. Do laundry	1	2	3	4	5	NA
15. Find important things (such as bills, tax forms, and so forth)	1	2	3	4	5	NA
16. Care for animals	1	2	3	4	5	NA

continued

B. Living Conditions

Please circle the number that best indicates how much of a problem you have with the following conditions in your home.

Problems in the home	None	A little	Somewhat/ moderate	Substantial	Severe
17. Structural damage (floors, walls, roof, and so on)	1	2	3	4	5
18. Presence of rotten food items	1	2	3	4	5
19. Insect infestation	1	2	3	4	5
20. Presence of human urine or feces	1	2	3	4	5
21. Presence of animal urine or feces	1	2	3	4	5
22. Water not working	1	2	3	4	5
23. Heat not working	1	2	3	4	5

C. Safety Issues

Please indicate whether you have any concerns about your home like those described in the following table.

Type of problem	Not at all	A little	Somewhat/ Moderate	Substantial	Severe
24. Does any part of your house pose a fire hazard? Consider, for example, a stove covered with paper, flammable objects near the furnace, and so forth.	1	2	3	4	5
25. Are parts of your house unsanitary? Are the bathrooms unclean? Is there a strong odor?	1	2	3	4	5
26. Would medical emergency personnel have difficulty moving equipment through your home?	1	2	3	4	5
27. Are any exits from your home blocked?	1	2	3	4	5
28. Is it unsafe to move up or down the stairs or along other walkways?	1	2	3	4	5
29. Is there clutter outside your house, such as in your porch, yard, alleyway, or common areas (if you live in an apartment or condo)?	1	2	3	4	5

these one more time helps you and your clinician see how much change has occurred in all areas related to hoarding.

Continuing Treatment on Your Own

It is likely that your therapist will begin tapering your treatment sessions so they occur less frequently. During the weeks between sessions, you should begin a self-therapy plan. We suggest you schedule self-sessions on the same day and time slot when meetings with your clinician usually occurred. Schedule your self-sessions ahead of time and mark them on your calendar. Your clinician will work with you to develop a formal plan for your self-sessions. This will be the time to practice sorting and not acquiring using the methods you found most helpful during treatment.

Booster Sessions

Because many people need time to establish new habits, you and your clinician may wish to schedule two or three "booster sessions" a few months apart. These sessions can help you reconnect with your goals to eliminate hoarding problems and remind you of treatment techniques you may have forgotten. You and your clinician can decide whether you need these sessions and how far apart they should be. Or you might decide that you will call your clinician to set up a time whenever you feel you need a little more help.

Review Treatment Techniques

Reviewing the treatment techniques you've been using is a critical activity for preventing relapse and helps remind you of what you have learned. Begin by reviewing the compulsive hoarding and acquiring models developed early during your treatment (chapter 3). Ask yourself whether these models are still accurate and whether you would make any changes to them now.

Next, remind yourself of your original treatment goals by examining the Goals Form you completed during the treatment planning phase (chapter 4). Review what you have actually accomplished, including changes in symp-

Table 9.1 List of Treatment Techniques

Identify the methods below that worked best for you. Many of these apply not only to letting go of possessions, but also to resisting acquiring and to organizing.

Review the model for understanding compulsive hoarding.

Identify your beliefs and emotions by

- Using the Downward Arrow Form.
- Using Thought Records.
- Visualizing the situation.
- Considering beliefs about comfort, loss, mistakes, identity, responsibility, memory, control.

Review your values.

Review your Treatment Goals.

Use an Organizing Plan:

- Keep supplies on hand for organizing.
- Only handle it once (OHIO).
- Keep decisions simple: Trash, recycle, sell, donate, keep.
- Use an egg-timer to make decisions faster.
- Implement decisions as soon as possible.
- Review questions for deciding on categories.
- Stick to your Organizing Plan and filing system.
- Schedule times to organize and file.
- Keep surfaces clear to prevent re-cluttering.

Review the Rules for Acquiring.

Review list of questions about organizing, acquiring, and letting go.

Review Problematic Thinking Styles about organizing, acquiring, and letting go.

Evaluate emotional thinking.

Evaluate capacity to cope.

List the advantages and disadvantages of acquiring or discarding.

Use cognitive strategies:

- Evaluate actual threat.
- Examine the evidence.
- Conduct a behavioral experiment to test your beliefs and predictions.
- Imagine the worst.
- Take another perspective: friend's view, your view of others (double standard), advice to others.
- Value your time.
- Evaluate need versus want.

Gradually practice to reduce discomfort and gain skill in:

- Resisting acquiring.
- Organizing.
- Letting go.

Practice problem-solving skills.

Plan social activities outside your home.

Invite others to visit you at home.

Schedule self-treatment sessions.

toms (e.g., acquiring, clutter, ability to get rid of things) as well as skills developed (organizing, resisting impulses to acquire, problem solving, managing attention).

Then, review the techniques learned during therapy by going over your Personal Session Forms and other material in this workbook. Review the list of treatment techniques presented in table 9.1 and keep it handy for future use.

Dealing with Setbacks

If you experience setbacks in dealing with clutter, getting rid of items, and urges to acquire, there are various strategies you can use to get back on track. For example, you can call your clinician and set up an appointment if you need it, you can seek help from a friend or coach, and you can review your treatment notes. Remember to use cognitive strategies to avoid catastrophizing about the problem you have encountered. Also remember to use your problem-solving skills to deal with even serious problems you encounter.

Homework

✎ Review your workbook and make a list of all the methods you've learned and highlight those you found most helpful.

✎ Review the list of skills to make a revised list of the ones that work best for you.

✎ Try out some skills you have not practiced for a while.

Conclusion

Congratulations! You are well on you way to overcoming your compulsive hoarding problem. With patience and continued effort, you will be able to maintain your progress and make even more gains. Keep in mind that you have vulnerabilities that led to your hoarding in the first place. These emotional and behavioral habits are part of you, but like most people, you can overcome them so you have control over your behavior. Your best allies in the struggle against tendencies to acquire and save too many things are your new skills and your social supports, including your clinician, and family members and friends who are supportive.

Appendix: Forms

Personal Session Form

Initials: _____   Session #: _____   Date: _____

Agenda:

_____

_____

_____

Main Points:

_____

_____

_____

_____

_____

Homework:

_____

_____

To discuss next time:

_____

_____

_____

_____

Intervention strategies used or reviewed:

_____

_____

_____

_____

Personal Session Form

Initials: _____   Session #: _____   Date: _____

Agenda:

_____

_____

_____

Main Points:

_____

_____

_____

_____

_____

_____

Homework:

_____

_____

To discuss next time:

_____

_____

_____

_____

Intervention strategies used or reviewed:

_____

_____

_____

_____

Personal Session Form

Initials: _____ Session #: _____ Date: _____

Agenda:

_____

_____

_____

Main Points:

_____

_____

_____

_____

_____

_____

Homework:

_____

_____

To discuss next time:

_____

_____

_____

_____

Intervention strategies used or reviewed:

_____

_____

_____

_____

Personal Session Form

Initials: _____   Session #: _____   Date: _____

Agenda:

_____

_____

_____

Main Points:

_____

_____

_____

_____

_____

_____

Homework:

_____

_____

To discuss next time:

_____

_____

_____

_____

Intervention strategies used or reviewed:

_____

_____

_____

_____

Personal Session Form

Initials: _____ Session #: _____ Date: _____

Agenda:

_____

_____

_____

Main Points:

_____

_____

_____

_____

_____

_____

Homework:

_____

_____

To discuss next time:

_____

_____

_____

_____

Intervention strategies used or reviewed:

_____

_____

_____

_____

Personal Session Form

Initials: _____   Session #: _____   Date: _____

Agenda:

_____

_____

Main Points:

_____

_____

_____

_____

_____

Homework:

_____

_____

To discuss next time:

_____

_____

_____

_____

Intervention strategies used or reviewed:

_____

_____

_____

_____

Personal Session Form

Initials: _____ Session #: _____ Date: _____

Agenda:

_____

_____

_____

Main Points:

_____

_____

_____

_____

_____

_____

Homework:

_____

_____

To discuss next time:

_____

_____

_____

_____

Intervention strategies used or reviewed:

_____

_____

_____

_____

Personal Session Form

Initials: _____ Session #: _____ Date: _____

Agenda:

_____

_____

_____

Main Points:

_____

_____

_____

_____

_____

_____

Homework:

_____

_____

To discuss next time:

_____

_____

_____

_____

Intervention strategies used or reviewed:

_____

_____

_____

_____

Personal Session Form

Initials: _____   Session #: _____   Date: _____

Agenda:

_____

_____

_____

Main Points:

_____

_____

_____

_____

_____

_____

Homework:

_____

_____

To discuss next time:

_____

_____

_____

_____

Intervention strategies used or reviewed:

_____

_____

_____

_____

Personal Session Form

Initials: _____ Session #: _____ Date: _____

Agenda:

_____

_____

_____

Main Points:

_____

_____

_____

_____

_____

Homework:

_____

_____

To discuss next time:

_____

_____

_____

_____

Intervention strategies used or reviewed:

_____

_____

_____

_____

Personal Session Form

Initials: _____   Session #: _____   Date: _____

Agenda:

_____

_____

_____

Main Points:

_____

_____

_____

_____

_____

_____

Homework:

_____

_____

To discuss next time:

_____

_____

_____

_____

Intervention strategies used or reviewed:

_____

_____

_____

_____

Personal Session Form

Initials: _____ Session #: _____ Date: _____

Agenda:

_____

_____

_____

Main Points:

_____

_____

_____

_____

_____

Homework:

_____

_____

To discuss next time:

_____

_____

_____

_____

Intervention strategies used or reviewed:

_____

_____

_____

_____

Personal Session Form

Initials: _____   Session #: _____   Date: _____

Agenda:

_____

_____

_____

Main Points:

_____

_____

_____

_____

_____

_____

Homework:

_____

_____

To discuss next time:

_____

_____

_____

_____

_____

Intervention strategies used or reviewed:

_____

_____

_____

_____

Personal Session Form

Initials: _____   Session #: _____   Date: _____

Agenda:

_____

_____

_____

Main Points:

_____

_____

_____

_____

_____

Homework:

_____

_____

To discuss next time:

_____

_____

_____

_____

Intervention strategies used or reviewed:

_____

_____

_____

_____

Personal Session Form

Initials: _____ Session #: _____ Date: _____

Agenda:

_____

_____

_____

Main Points:

_____

_____

_____

_____

_____

_____

Homework:

_____

_____

To discuss next time:

_____

_____

_____

_____

Intervention strategies used or reviewed:

_____

_____

_____

_____

Personal Session Form

Initials: _____ Session #: _____ Date: _____

Agenda:

_____

_____

_____

Main Points:

_____

_____

_____

_____

_____

_____

Homework:

_____

_____

To discuss next time:

_____

_____

_____

_____

Intervention strategies used or reviewed:

_____

_____

_____

_____

Brief Thought Record

Initials: _____   Date: _____

Trigger situation	Thought or belief	Emotions	Actions/behaviors

Brief Thought Record

Initials: _____   Date: _____

Trigger situation	Thought or belief	Emotions	Actions/behaviors

Brief Thought Record

Initials: _____   Date: _____

Trigger situation	Thought or belief	Emotions	Actions/behaviors

Downward Arrow Form

Item: _____

In thinking about getting rid of (discarding, recycling, selling, giving away) this, what thoughts occur to you?

_____

_____

_____

If you got rid of this, what do you think would happen?

_____

_____

_____

If this were true, why would it be so upsetting? (What would it mean to you? Why would that be so bad?)

_____

_____

_____

If that were true, what's so bad about that?

_____

_____

_____

What's the worst part about that?

_____

_____

_____

What does that mean about *you?*

_____

_____

_____

_____

Downward Arrow Form

Item: _____

In thinking about getting rid of (discarding, recycling, selling, giving away) this, what thoughts occur to you?

_____

_____

_____

If you got rid of this, what do you think would happen?

_____

_____

_____

If this were true, why would it be so upsetting? (What would it mean to you? Why would that be so bad?)

_____

_____

_____

If that were true, what's so bad about that?

_____

_____

_____

What's the worst part about that?

_____

_____

_____

What does that mean about *you?*

_____

_____

_____

_____

Downward Arrow Form

Item: _____

In thinking about getting rid of (discarding, recycling, selling, giving away) this, what thoughts occur to you?

_____

_____

_____

If you got rid of this, what do you think would happen?

_____

_____

_____

If this were true, why would it be so upsetting? (What would it mean to you? Why would that be so bad?)

_____

_____

_____

If that were true, what's so bad about that?

_____

_____

_____

What's the worst part about that?

_____

_____

_____

What does that mean about *you?*

_____

_____

_____

_____

Practice Form

A. What was the item (to remove or not to acquire)? _____

_____

Initial discomfort (0 = no discomfort to 10 = maximal discomfort) _____

_____

_____

B. What did you do (not acquire, trash, recycle, give away, other)? _____

_____

_____

_____

Discomfort rating (0 to 10)   after 10 min   _____

after 20 min   _____

after 30 min   _____

after 40 min   _____

after 50 min   _____

after 1 hour   _____

the next day   _____

C. Conclusion regarding experiment: _____

_____

_____

_____

_____

_____

_____

_____

Practice Form

A. What was the item (to remove or not to acquire)? _____

_____

Initial discomfort (0 = no discomfort to 10 = maximal discomfort) _____

_____

_____

B. What did you do (not acquire, trash, recycle, give away, other)? _____

_____

_____

_____

Discomfort rating (0 to 10)   after 10 min   _____

after 20 min   _____

after 30 min   _____

after 40 min   _____

after 50 min   _____

after 1 hour   _____

the next day   _____

C. Conclusion regarding experiment: _____

_____

_____

_____

_____

_____

Practice Form

A. What was the item (to remove or not to acquire)? _____

_____

Initial discomfort (0 = no discomfort to 10 = maximal discomfort) _____

_____

_____

B. What did you do (not acquire, trash, recycle, give away, other)? _____

_____

_____

_____

Discomfort rating (0 to 10)   after 10 min   _____

                                   after 20 min   _____

                                   after 30 min   _____

                                   after 40 min   _____

                                   after 50 min   _____

                                   after 1 hour   _____

                                   the next day   _____

C. Conclusion regarding experiment: _____

_____

_____

_____

_____

_____

_____

Practice Form

A. What was the item (to remove or not to acquire)? _____

_____

Initial discomfort (0 = no discomfort to 10 = maximal discomfort) _____

_____

_____

B. What did you do (not acquire, trash, recycle, give away, other)? _____

_____

_____

_____

Discomfort rating (0 to 10)   after 10 min _____

after 20 min _____

after 30 min _____

after 40 min _____

after 50 min _____

after 1 hour _____

the next day _____

C. Conclusion regarding experiment: _____

_____

_____

_____

_____

_____

_____

Practice Form

A. What was the item (to remove or not to acquire)? _____

_____

Initial discomfort (0 = no discomfort to 10 = maximal discomfort) _____

_____

_____

B. What did you do (not acquire, trash, recycle, give away, other)? _____

_____

_____

_____

Discomfort rating (0 to 10)   after 10 min _____

after 20 min _____

after 30 min _____

after 40 min _____

after 50 min _____

after 1 hour _____

the next day _____

C. Conclusion regarding experiment: _____

_____

_____

_____

_____

_____

_____

Practice Form

A. What was the item (to remove or not to acquire)? _____

_____

Initial discomfort (0 = no discomfort to 10 = maximal discomfort) _____

_____

_____

B. What did you do (not acquire, trash, recycle, give away, other)? _____

_____

_____

_____

Discomfort rating (0 to 10)   after 10 min   _____

after 20 min   _____

after 30 min   _____

after 40 min   _____

after 50 min   _____

after 1 hour   _____

the next day   _____

C. Conclusion regarding experiment: _____

_____

_____

_____

_____

_____

_____

Task List

Priority Rating	Task	Date Put on List	Date Completed
A			
•			
•			
•			
•			
•			
•			
B			
•			
•			
•			
•			
•			
•			
C			
•			
•			
•			
•			
•			
•			

Task List

Priority Rating	Task	Date Put on List	Date Completed
A			
•			
•			
•			
•			
•			
B			
•			
•			
•			
•			
•			
C			
•			
•			
•			
•			
•			

Task List

Priority Rating	Task	Date Put on List	Date Completed
A			
•			
•			
•			
•			
•			
B			
•			
•			
•			
•			
•			
•			
C			
•			
•			
•			
•			
•			
•			

Task List

Priority Rating	Task	Date Put on List	Date Completed
A			
•			
•			
•			
•			
•			
B			
•			
•			
•			
•			
•			
•			
C			
•			
•			
•			
•			
•			
•			

Task List

Priority Rating	Task	Date Put on List	Date Completed
A			
•			
•			
•			
•			
•			
•			
B			
•			
•			
•			
•			
•			
•			
C			
•			
•			
•			
•			
•			
•			

Behavioral Experiment Form

Initials: _____   Date: _____

1. Behavioral experiment to be completed: _____

_____

_____

2. What do you predict (are afraid) will happen? _____

_____

_____

_____

3. How strongly do you believe this will happen (0–100%)? _____

_____

4. Initial discomfort (0–10) _____

5. What actually happened? _____

_____

_____

_____

_____

6. Final discomfort (0–10) _____

7. Did your predictions come true? _____

8. What conclusions do you draw from this experiment? _____

_____

_____

_____

_____

Behavioral Experiment Form

Initials: _____   Date: _____

1. Behavioral experiment to be completed: _____

_____

_____

2. What do you predict (are afraid) will happen? _____

_____

_____

_____

3. How strongly do you believe this will happen (0–100%)? _____

_____

4. Initial discomfort (0–10) _____

5. What actually happened? _____

_____

_____

_____

_____

6. Final discomfort (0–10) _____

7. Did your predictions come true? _____

8. What conclusions do you draw from this experiment? _____

_____

_____

_____

_____

Behavioral Experiment Form

Initials: _____   Date: _____

1. Behavioral experiment to be completed: _____

   _____

   _____

2. What do you predict (are afraid) will happen? _____

   _____

   _____

   _____

3. How strongly do you believe this will happen (0–100%)? _____

   _____

4. Initial discomfort (0–10) _____

5. What actually happened? _____

   _____

   _____

   _____

   _____

6. Final discomfort (0–10) _____

7. Did your predictions come true? _____

8. What conclusions do you draw from this experiment? _____

   _____

   _____

   _____

   _____

Behavioral Experiment Form

Initials: _____   Date: _____

1. Behavioral experiment to be completed: _____

_____

_____

2. What do you predict (are afraid) will happen? _____

_____

_____

_____

3. How strongly do you believe this will happen (0–100%)? _____

_____

4. Initial discomfort (0–10) _____

5. What actually happened? _____

_____

_____

_____

_____

6. Final discomfort (0–10) _____

7. Did your predictions come true? _____

8. What conclusions do you draw from this experiment? _____

_____

_____

_____

_____

Behavioral Experiment Form

Initials: _____   Date: _____

1. Behavioral experiment to be completed: _____

   _____

   _____

2. What do you predict (are afraid) will happen? _____

   _____

   _____

   _____

3. How strongly do you believe this will happen (0–100%)? _____

   _____

4. Initial discomfort (0–10) _____

5. What actually happened? _____

   _____

   _____

   _____

   _____

6. Final discomfort (0–10) _____

7. Did your predictions come true? _____

8. What conclusions do you draw from this experiment? _____

   _____

   _____

   _____

   _____

Thought Record

Initials: _____   Date: _____

Trigger item or question	Automatic thought or belief	Emotions	Rational alternative (note and cognitive errors)	Outcome

Thought Record

Initials: _____   Date: _____

Trigger item or question	Automatic thought or belief	Emotions	Rational alternative (note and cognitive errors)	Outcome

Thought Record

Initials: _____ Date: _____

Trigger item or question	Automatic thought or belief	Emotions	Rational alternative (note and cognitive errors)	Outcome

Thought Record

Initials: _____   Date: _____

Trigger item or question	Automatic thought or belief	Emotions	Rational alternative (note and cognitive errors)	Outcome

Thought Record

Initials: _____   Date: _____

Trigger item or question	Automatic thought or belief	Emotions	Rational alternative (note and cognitive errors)	Outcome

About the Authors

Gail Steketee, PhD, is professor and currently dean *ad interim* at the Boston University School of Social Work. She received her MSW and PhD from Bryn Mawr Graduate School of Social Work and Social Research. Dr. Steketee has conducted a variety of research studies on the psychopathology and treatment of obsessive–compulsive and related spectrum disorders. Her recent research, funded by the National Institute of Mental Health, focuses on diagnostic and personality aspects of compulsive hoarding, and tests a specialized cognitive and behavioral treatment for this condition. Additional funded research interests include cognitive therapy for obsessive–compulsive disorder (OCD), developing treatment for body dysmorphic disorder, and familial factors that influence treatment outcomes for OCD and panic with agoraphobia. She is also a member of the Hoarding of Animals Research Consortium, which studies compulsive hoarding of animals. Drs. Steketee and Frost co-chair an international research group—the Obsessive–Compulsive Cognitions Working Group—dedicated to the study of cognitive aspects of OCD. She has published more than 150 journal articles, chapters, and books on OCD and related disorders, including *When Once Is Not Enough* (1990), *Treatment for Obsessive–Compulsive Disorder* (1993), *Overcoming Obsessive–Compulsive Disorder* (1993), and with Dr. Frost, *Cognitive Approaches to Obsessive–Compulsive Disorder: Theory, Assessment and Treatment* (2002). Upcoming books that she has co-authored on OCD and compulsive hoarding include *Cognitive Therapy for Obsessive Compulsive Disorder* (2006) and *Buried in Treasures: A Self-Help Guide for Compulsive Hoarding* (Oxford University Press, 2006).

Randy O. Frost, PhD, received his degree in clinical psychology from the University of Kansas in 1977 after completing his doctoral internship at the University of Washington School of Medicine. Currently he holds the Harold Edward and Elsa Siipola Israel Professorship at Smith College. He has published more than 100 scientific articles and book chapters on OCD and compulsive hoarding, as well as on the pathology of perfectionism and related topics. With Gail Steketee he has co-edited one book, *Cognitive Approaches to Obsessions and Compulsions: Theory, Assessment, and Treatment* (2002), and has another upcoming, *Buried in Treasures: A Self-Help Guide for Compulsive Hoarding* (Oxford University Press, 2006).

Dr. Frost co-edits the Obsessive Compulsive Foundation (OCF) website on hoarding, and serves on the OCF Scientific Advisory Board. Together with Dr. Steketee he is co-coordinator of an international group of researchers studying beliefs in OCD—the Obsessive–Compulsive Cognitions Working Group. He is also a member of the Hoarding of Animals Research Consortium and has been consultant to various hoarding task forces, including those in New York, New York; Ottawa, Canada; and Hampden, Hampshire, and Franklin counties in Massachusetts. He has given hundreds of lectures and workshops on the topic of hoarding nationally and internationally. His research on hoarding has been supported by the National Institute of Mental Health and the OCF.